New and Revised

Big, Soft, Chewy

COOKIES

More Than 75 Recipes for the Best Cookies in the World

Jill Van Cleave

Contemporary Books

Chicago   New York   San Francisco   Lisbon   London   Madrid   Mexico City
Milan   New Delhi   San Juan   Seoul   Singapore   Sydney   Toronto

The **McGraw·Hill** Companies

Library of Congress Cataloging-in-Publication Data

Van Cleave, Jill.
    Big, soft, chewy cookies : more than 75 recipes for the best cookies in the
world / Jill Van Cleave.—new and revised ed.
        p.   cm.
    ISBN 0-07-141866-0
    1. Cookies.   I. Title.

TX772.V26   2003
641.8'654—dc21   2003043820

For the kid in all of us

1 2 3 4 5 6 7 8 9 0   LBM/LBM   2 1 0 9 8 7 6 5 4 3

ISBN 0-07-141866-0

Interior design by Diane Jaroch

McGraw-Hill books are available at special quantity discounts to use as premiums and
sales promotions, or for use in corporate training programs. For more information, please
write to the Director of Special Sales, Professional Publishing, McGraw-Hill, Two Penn
Plaza, New York, NY 10121-2298. Or contact your local bookstore.

This book is printed on acid-free paper.

Contents

Acknowledgments

A special thank you with fond remembrance goes to my late agent, Barry Bluestein.

I am grateful every day for my husband, Bill, who ate his way through the first book and was again up to the task for this edition.

Introduction

What is the best way to satisfy the urge for a tasty treat, a mouthwatering aroma, and a warm fuzzy feeling all at the same time? Why, with a cookie, of course! And, as we all know, the best warm fuzzies come from the best kind of cookie—big, soft, and chewy, with blissful textures and sweet surprises, and full of tender crumbs.

The cookies we remember from childhood, the ones that gave us such pleasure and gratification, were not tiny, thin, bland wafers. They were cookie-jar cookies—big enough to fill two small hands, soft enough to wash down with a glass of milk, and chewy enough to let us savor the intoxicating flavor of each delectable bite. Big, soft cookies are nurturing cookies. They are the ones we wish to treat ourselves, our children, and our children's children to.

This edition is revised and updated to include almost twenty new recipes. Some of these are contemporary twists on old favorites such as the Nearly Biscotti, others are classic like the Cinnamon Walnut Rugelach or fruity as in the Rhubarb Oat Bar Cookie. Still others, like my Vanilla Cream Sandwich Cookies, have been added for the sheer fun of eating them. The book is divided by cookie types—drop cookies, shaped cookies, bar cookies, and holiday cookies.

Drop cookies are the simplest to make and require the least amount of time to prepare. With these recipes, all you usually have to do is mix the dough, scoop it up in spoonfuls, drop it onto a cookie sheet, and bake. Sometimes you must scoop and roll the dough before placing it onto the cookie sheet, but that is as complicated as it gets to make them.

Exactly as you would expect, to make shaped cookies, you roll and cut the dough into shapes or slices, press it out of a pastry bag, or shape it by using a mold. These cookie doughs often require chilling before you shape and bake them.

Bar cookies are baked in square or rectangular baking pans. Brownies are bar cookies, as are layered cookies with a bottom crust and topping or a filling sandwiched between two crusts. Bar cookies require a little more time to bake than drop cookies, but they take no extra effort.

The festive holiday cookie recipes include temptations such as spirited Eggnog Cookies with Rum Butter Icing; rich shortbread slices covered with almond caramel; and decadent three-layered Chocolate Truffle Triangles. In addition, you'll find recipes for timeless favorites like Classic Chocolate Chip Cookies; seasonal treats including Ginger Cookies; traditional goodies such as Super Duper Snickerdoodles; and bold, new delights like my Brown Butter Pecan Cookies.

I urge you to try all of these recipes. After all, while it may be possible to live by oatmeal raisin cookies alone, why limit yourself to just one soft, chewy taste of heaven?

Tips for Handling, Baking, and Storing Soft Cookies

As easy as soft cookies are to prepare, it is possible to meet defeat. The dough can be mishandled, a cookie can bake hard in the oven, or the cookies can be incorrectly stored if the baker is not aware of these few tips that guarantee success:

• When mixing cookie dough, do not overbeat it once the dry ingredients have been added. Mix just until the flour has been incorporated into the dough. Overworking the dough will toughen the cookie.

• When you are making shaped cookies, if the dough is too soft to handle, chill it (in a tightly sealed container) for at least an hour before forming cookies.

• Most cookie dough, with the exception of bar cookies and macaroons, may be stored in a tightly sealed container in the refrigerator for up to three days. Freeze dough for up to two months unless otherwise indicated in the recipe. Thaw in the refrigerator before using.

• Make sure that your oven is correctly calibrated. Baking cookies at the wrong temperature is a sure way to either undercook or burn them.

• Use stainless steel or aluminum cookie sheets to bake cookies. Very dark colored pans may cause cookies to overheat and possibly burn. Battleship gray, however, is acceptable. Using insulated cookie sheets may take longer in the oven and can result in a softer cookie texture than intended.

- Nonstick baking sheets are excellent for any cookie that requires greased pans. Parchment paper, cut to fit baking sheets, makes a good nonstick surface and can be discarded after baking for easy cleanup. Nonstick baking mats made of woven rubberized silicone are perfect for cookie baking. They provide even heat distribution and are simple to use, easy to clean, and reusable.

- Do not overbake cookies. Remember that cookies will continue to bake on cookie sheets out of oven. Transfer baked cookies to cooling rack as soon as they have firmed.

- Cookies harden naturally as they sit out over time. If you want your cookies soft, consume them within three days. Some cookies become stale faster than others and will need to be stored in an airtight plastic storage bag or wrapped individually in plastic wrap to prevent hardening. Storage directions are indicated in the recipes. In general, store cookies at room temperature, not in the refrigerator.

- Cookies with a high moisture content, especially cookies made with pureed fruit, should not be stored in airtight containers. The moisture in these cookies will cause them to become unpleasantly gummy. After these cookies have cooled, place them on a plate, and loosely cover the plate with a cloth towel or napkin. To hide cookies from kids and pets, put them into a paper-towel-lined cardboard shoe box with lid.

- Most of these cookies freeze beautifully once baked, and they will be soft and yummy when you bring them back to room temperature. Freeze cookies for up to three months in plastic freezer bags or tight fitting containers. Do not freeze frosted cookies; ice them after they have thawed.

More Tips for the Curious Cook

Experienced bakers generally have inquisitive minds. Have you ever wondered what ingredients contribute to producing soft cookies? Here are some general tips that can be applied to your cookie-baking repertoire:

- Soft-cookie doughs usually have more moisture than doughs for crisp cookies. If your soft-cookie dough looks dry, add an egg or a small amount of a liquid dairy ingredient such as milk, cream, buttermilk, or sour cream.

- Incorporate pureed fruit into a cookie dough for added moisture and flavor. High-moisture dried fruits, such as figs, dates, and dried plums, can soften otherwise dry cookies.

- The addition of cake flour will give a more tender crumb to the baked cookie than using all-purpose flour for the total amount. Bleached all-purpose flour is softer (less protein) than unbleached and preferable for making cookies.

- Excess sugar in the dough often results in crisp—not soft—cookies. If you like your cookies soft but very sweet, you can frost them once they are baked and cooled.

- Unsalted butter is used for its fresh, clean taste and rich flavor. If salted butter is substituted, eliminate the salt from the recipe. Butter will soften to room temperature for creaming purposes within one hour on warm days or might take twice as long in cooler kitchens. Room temperature butter (65 to 75°F) should give easily when pressed.

I

Drop COOKIES

A wonderful almond flavor permeates
this soft cookie, leaving a delicate aftertaste
that lingers in the memory.

Almond Cookies

1 cup (2 sticks) unsalted butter, at room temperature

1 cup granulated sugar

2 large eggs

1 cup canned almond filling (see Note)

¼ cup whole milk

3 cups all-purpose flour

½ teaspoon baking soda

¼ teaspoon salt

¼ cup sliced blanched almonds

NOTE: Almond filling is available in ready-to-use 12-ounce cans in most supermarkets.

1. Heat oven to 350°F.

2. In a mixing bowl, cream butter and sugar until smooth. Add eggs and blend. Add almond filling and milk and blend again.

3. In a separate bowl, mix flour, baking soda, and salt. Add to the creamed mixture.

4. Scoop 2 rounded tablespoons of dough and roll to form each cookie. Drop dough onto lightly greased or nonstick cookie sheets, spacing the cookies 2 inches apart. Press sliced almonds onto tops.

5. Bake until cookies are lightly golden and firm to the touch, about 15 minutes. Using a spatula, transfer cookies to a rack and let cool.

Makes about 28 cookies.

Store cookies in an airtight jar or tin at room temperature for up to three days. Do not freeze dough.

The spicy, earthy flavors in this soft, cakelike cookie are universally appealing. Bring these along on picnics, to tailgate parties, or as a box-lunch treat.

Applesauce Cranberry Cookies

1 cup dried cranberries (see Note)

2½ cups all-purpose flour

1 teaspoon allspice

½ teaspoon baking soda

½ teaspoon salt

½ cup (1 stick) unsalted butter, at room temperature

1 cup packed dark brown sugar

1 cup natural applesauce (no sugar added)

NOTE: **You may substitute currants for the dried cranberries, if desired.**

1   Soak cranberries in warm water for 15 minutes to soften. Drain and set aside.

2   Combine flour, allspice, baking soda, and salt in a bowl. Set aside.

3   In a mixing bowl, cream butter and sugar until fluffy and smooth. Add applesauce and blend.

4   Stir in flour mixture and cranberries. Cover bowl with plastic wrap and refrigerate for at least one hour.

5   Heat oven to 375°F.

6   Using either an individual ¼-cup measure or a 2-ounce ice-cream scoop, scoop level amounts of dough and drop 2 inches apart onto ungreased cookie sheets.

7   Bake until cookies are firm to the touch, about 15 minutes. Using a spatula, transfer cookies to a rack and let cool.

Makes about 16 cookies.

Store cookies in a loosely covered container at room temperature for up to three days.

Ripe bananas provide rich fruit
flavor to this soft, iced cookie.

Banana Blitz Cookies

¾ cup (1½ sticks) unsalted butter, at room temperature

1 cup packed light brown sugar

1 cup mashed ripe banana (about 2 bananas)

½ teaspoon banana extract

2 cups all-purpose flour

½ teaspoon mace

¼ teaspoon baking soda

¼ teaspoon salt

1 cup coarsely chopped toasted pecans

White Icing (recipe follows)

1 Heat oven to 375°F.

2 In a mixing bowl, cream butter and sugar until fluffy and smooth. Add
     mashed banana and extract and blend.

3   In a separate bowl, mix flour, mace, baking soda, and salt. Add to the creamed mixture. Stir in pecans.

4   Using an individual ¼-cup measure or a 2-ounce ice-cream scoop, scoop level amounts of dough and drop 2 inches apart onto ungreased cookie sheets.

5   Bake until cookies are firm to the touch, about 15 minutes. Using a spatula, transfer cookies to a rack and let cool.

6   Ice cookies after they have completely cooled.

Makes about 16 cookies.

Store cookies in a loosely covered container at room temperature for up to three days.

WHITE ICING	1 cup confectioners' sugar
	4–5 teaspoons milk

1   Using a fork, mix sugar and milk together, adding one teaspoon of milk at a time to produce a smooth, thick icing that falls from the fork in a slow stream.

2   Drizzle icing over tops of cooled cookies. Let icing harden before serving.

Black walnuts are little treasures in the baking chest of
good ingredients. These wonderful gems (and sweet butter)
give this extra-large cookie its deep, distinctive taste.

Black Walnut Butter Cookies

1 cup (2 sticks) unsalted butter, at room temperature

¾ cup packed light brown sugar

2 large eggs

1 teaspoon vanilla extract

2 cups all-purpose flour

½ teaspoon baking soda

½ teaspoon salt

1 cup chopped black walnuts

1   Heat oven to 350°F.

2   In a mixing bowl, cream butter and sugar until fluffy and smooth. Add eggs and vanilla and blend.

3   In a separate bowl, mix flour, baking soda, and salt. Add to creamed mixture. Stir in walnuts.

4   Using either an individual ¼-cup measure or a 2-ounce ice-cream scoop, scoop level amounts of dough and drop 3 inches apart onto ungreased cookie sheets.

5   Bake until cookies are golden brown, about 15 minutes. Using a spatula, transfer cookies to a rack and let cool.

Makes about 14 cookies.

Store cookies in an airtight jar or tin at room temperature for up to three days.

In this tasty cookie, the combination of toasted pecans and butter melted until golden brown results in a delectable taste sensation reminiscent of pralines. This dough may be used immediately or covered with plastic wrap and refrigerated for up to four hours before baking.

Brown Butter Pecan Cookies

1 cup coarsely chopped pecans

¾ cup (1½ sticks) unsalted butter

1½ cups all-purpose flour

½ cup cake flour

¼ teaspoon baking soda

¼ teaspoon salt

2 large eggs

1 cup packed light brown sugar

½ teaspoon vanilla extract

1   Heat oven to 350°F.

2   Spread pecans in a baking dish and toast in oven for 10 minutes. Remove and set aside.

3   Melt butter in a skillet over medium-low heat until just browned (about 5 minutes). (Be careful not to let it burn.) Immediately remove from heat and transfer to a small bowl to stop the cooking. Set aside to cool.

4   In a bowl, mix both flours with the baking soda and salt.

5   In a separate large bowl, beat eggs and sugar until smooth. Add vanilla; then add cooled browned butter and blend. Stir in the flour mixture and toasted pecans.

6   Using either an individual ¼-cup measure or a 2-ounce ice-cream scoop, scoop level amounts of dough and drop 2½ inches apart onto greased or nonstick cookie sheets.

7   Bake until cookies are golden brown and firm to the touch, about 15 minutes. Using a spatula, transfer cookies to a rack and let cool.

Makes about 12 cookies.

Store cookies in an airtight plastic storage bag or wrap cookies individually in plastic wrap and store at room temperature for up to three days.

A simple-looking cookie that packs
a drop-dead rich, butterscotch taste.
This is definitely a crowd pleaser.

Butterscotch Cookies

1 cup (2 sticks) unsalted butter, at room temperature

1½ cups packed dark brown sugar

1 large egg

3 tablespoons whipping cream

1 teaspoon vanilla extract

2 cups all-purpose flour

1 cup cake flour

1 teaspoon baking soda

½ teaspoon salt

1   Heat oven to 375°F.

2   In a mixing bowl, cream butter and sugar until smooth. Add the egg, whipping cream, and vanilla and blend.

3   In a separate bowl, mix both flours with the baking soda and salt. Add to creamed mixture.

4   Using either an individual ¼-cup measure or a 2-ounce ice-cream scoop, scoop level amounts of dough and drop 2 inches apart onto ungreased cookie sheets.

5   Bake until cookies are golden and firm to the touch, about 15 minutes. Using a spatula, transfer cookies to a rack and let cool.

Makes about 16 cookies.

To prevent hardening, wrap each cookie individually in plastic wrap and store at room temperature for up to three days.

A thin, crisp crust envelops this very tender,
cardamom-scented cookie. It's wonderful with
a good strong cup of coffee in the morning.

Cardamom Buttermilk Cookies

½ cup (1 stick) unsalted butter, at room temperature

1 cup packed light brown sugar

1 large egg

½ cup buttermilk

2 cups all-purpose flour

1½ teaspoons cardamom

½ teaspoon baking soda

¼ teaspoon salt

1 Heat oven to 350°F.

2 In a mixing bowl, cream butter and sugar until smooth. Add egg and blend. Add buttermilk and blend again.

3 In a separate bowl, mix flour, cardamom, baking soda, and salt. Add to creamed mixture.

4 Scoop 2 rounded tablespoons of dough and roll to form each cookie. Drop dough onto ungreased cookie sheets, spacing 2 inches apart.

5 Bake until cookies are golden brown and firm to the touch, about 15 minutes. Using a spatula, transfer cookies to a rack and let cool.

Makes about 20 cookies.

Store cookies in an airtight plastic storage bag at room temperature for up to three days.

Sweet morsels of candied cherry
are hidden inside this soft cookie, rich
with chocolate and sour cream.

Chocolate Cherry Cookies

2 ounces unsweetened chocolate, cut into pieces

½ cup (1 stick) unsalted butter, at room temperature

1 cup packed dark brown sugar

1 large egg

1 teaspoon vanilla extract

½ cup sour cream

1½ cups all-purpose flour

½ teaspoon baking soda

¼ teaspoon salt

¾ cup coarsely chopped glacé red cherries

9 whole glacé red cherries for garnish

1 Heat oven to 350°F.

2 Melt chocolate in the top of a double boiler over barely simmering water. Or, place in a microwavable dish and melt in microwave set on medium power for 1 to 2 minutes. Stir until smooth and set aside.

3 In a mixing bowl, cream butter and sugar until smooth. Add egg and vanilla and blend. Add sour cream and blend again. Stir in melted chocolate.

4 In a separate bowl, mix 1 cup of flour, baking soda, and salt. Add to creamed mixture. In a small bowl, toss the remaining ½ cup flour with the chopped cherries. Stir into dough.

5 Scoop 2 rounded tablespoons dough and roll to form each cookie. Drop onto ungreased cookie sheets, spacing 2½ inches apart. Cut each whole cherry in half. Center one half onto each cookie.

6 Bake until cookies are just barely firm to the touch, about 15 minutes. Using a spatula, transfer cookies to a rack and let cool.

Makes about 18 cookies.

Store cookies in an airtight plastic storage bag at room temperature for up to three days.

Rich and seductive, with chocolate melting into even more chocolate, this cookie is impossible for any chocophile to resist.

Chocolate Chocolate Chip Cookies

2 ounces unsweetened chocolate, cut into pieces

½ cup (1 stick) unsalted butter, at room temperature

1 cup granulated sugar

1 large egg

¼ cup whole milk

1 teaspoon vanilla extract

2 cups all-purpose flour

1 teaspoon baking powder

¼ teaspoon salt

1 cup semisweet chocolate chips

1   Heat oven to 350°F.

2   Melt chocolate in the top of a double boiler over barely simmering water. Or, place in a microwavable dish and melt in microwave set on medium power for 1 to 2 minutes. Stir until smooth and set aside.

3   In a mixing bowl, cream butter and sugar until smooth. Add egg, milk, and vanilla and blend. Add melted chocolate and blend again.

4   In a separate bowl, mix flour, baking powder, and salt. Add to creamed mixture. Stir in chocolate chips.

5   Scoop dough into 1½-inch balls and drop 2 inches apart onto ungreased cookie sheets.

6   Bake until cookies are firm to the touch, about 15 minutes. Using a spatula, transfer cookies to a rack and let cool.

Makes about 18 cookies.

Store cookies in an airtight plastic storage bag at room temperature for up to five days.

Macaroons represent the very definition of chewy.
A thin crust on the outside yields to a soft,
chocolaty, chewy interior. Mmm, macaroons!

Chocolate Coconut Macaroons

6 ounces semisweet or bittersweet chocolate, cut into pieces

2 large egg whites

⅓ cup granulated sugar

1 teaspoon vanilla extract

2 cups sweetened shredded coconut

1   Heat oven to 350°F.

2   Melt chocolate in the top of a double boiler over barely simmering water. Or, place in a microwavable dish and melt in microwave set on medium power for 3 minutes. Stir until smooth and set aside to cool until barely warm.

3   Using an electric mixer, beat egg whites until frothy. Add sugar slowly, beating whites to soft peaks. Mix in vanilla. Stir in melted chocolate, then coconut.

4   Scoop rounded tablespoons of dough and drop 2 inches apart onto greased or nonstick cookie sheets.

5   Bake cookies until a thin outside crust forms, about 18 minutes. Remove cookies from oven and let them set for 5 minutes. Using a spatula, transfer cookies to a rack and let cool.

Makes about 18 cookies.

Store cookies in an airtight jar or tin at room temperature for up to three days.

Drop
COOKIES

Bite for bite, these cookies are incredibly intense.
They are loaded with chocolate and more chocolate
and finished with nutty walnuts for crunch.

Chocolate Fudgies

8 ounces semisweet chocolate, cut into pieces

1 cup all-purpose flour

¼ cup Dutch-processed cocoa powder

1 teaspoon baking powder

½ teaspoon salt

6 tablespoons (¾ stick) unsalted butter, at room temperature

1 cup granulated sugar

2 large eggs

1 teaspoon vanilla extract

1 teaspoon instant espresso powder

¾ cup real semisweet chocolate chips or chunks

1 cup coarsely chopped walnuts

22

1   Heat oven to 350°F.

2   Melt chocolate in the top of a double boiler over barely simmering water. Or, place in a microwavable dish and melt in microwave set on medium power for 3 minutes. Stir until smooth and set aside to cool.

3   Sift flour, cocoa, baking powder, and salt together in a bowl and set aside.

4   In a separate bowl, cream butter and sugar until smooth. Add eggs; then add vanilla and espresso powder and blend. Add melted chocolate and blend again. Stir in flour mixture, chocolate chips, and walnuts. (Dough will be stiff.)

5   Using either an individual ¼-cup measure or a 2-ounce ice-cream scoop, scoop level amounts of dough and drop 2 inches apart onto greased or nonstick cookie sheets.

6   Bake until cookies are dry on the outside but with soft centers, about 12 minutes. Remove cookies from oven and let them set for 3 minutes. Using a spatula, transfer cookies to a rack and let cool.

Makes about 18 cookies.

Store cookies in an airtight plastic storage bag at room temperature for up to three days.

This simple cookie has the haunting taste of malt that grows with each bite. Also, it has an unusual ingredient—softened ice cream— added to the dough that gives the cookie an extra creamy texture.

Chocolate Milkshake Cookies

½ cup chocolate ice cream (see Note)

½ cup (1 stick) unsalted butter, at room temperature

½ cup granulated sugar, plus ¼ cup for garnish

1 large egg

1 teaspoon vanilla extract

2 cups all-purpose flour

¼ cup chocolate malt powder

½ teaspoon baking powder

¼ teaspoon salt

NOTE: You may substitute vanilla ice cream for the chocolate, if desired, and use regular flavored malt powder with it.

1 Soften ice cream at room temperature until creamy but not melted.

2 In a mixing bowl, cream butter and ½ cup sugar until fluffy and smooth. Add egg and vanilla and blend. Add softened ice cream and blend again.

3 In a separate bowl, mix flour, malt powder, baking powder, and salt. Add to the creamed mixture. Cover dough with plastic wrap and refrigerate for at least 1 hour.

4 Heat oven to 375°F.

5 To form each cookie, roll 2 level tablespoons of chilled dough into a ball. Pour the remaining ¼ cup of sugar onto a plate. Roll each ball in the sugar to coat all sides. Place 2 inches apart on ungreased cookie sheets and flatten into 2½-inch rounds.

6 Bake until cookies are firm to the touch, about 15 minutes. Using a spatula, transfer cookies to a rack and let cool.

Makes about 16 cookies.

To prevent hardening, wrap each cookie individually in plastic wrap and store at room temperature for up to three days.

Candy makers aren't the only ones who can combine chocolate with mint for an unbeatable flavor. Try these for a special taste treat. A creamy icing provides the crowning touch.

Chocolate Mint Cookies

4 ounces bittersweet or semisweet chocolate, cut into pieces

½ cup (1 stick) unsalted butter, cut into pieces

1 cup packed light brown sugar

1 large egg

¼ cup whipping cream

1 teaspoon peppermint extract

1¾ cups cake flour

½ teaspoon baking powder

¼ teaspoon salt

Mint Cream Icing (See page 99.)

1   Heat oven to 350°F.

2   Melt chocolate and butter in the top of a double boiler over barely simmering water. Or, place in a microwavable dish and melt in microwave set on medium power for about 2 minutes, stirring occasionally. Set aside and let cool to room temperature.

3   In a mixing bowl, beat sugar and egg until blended. Add whipping cream and peppermint extract. Stir in cooled chocolate mixture and blend.

4   In a separate bowl, mix flour, baking powder, and salt. Add to creamed mixture.

5   Scoop 2 level tablespoons of dough and roll to form each cookie. Drop dough onto ungreased cookie sheets, spacing 2½ inches apart.

6   Bake until tops of cookies look crackled, about 12 minutes. (Cookies will still feel soft.) Using a spatula, transfer cookies to a rack and let cool.

7   When cookies have cooled completely, drizzle tops with Mint Cream Icing.

Makes about 18 cookies.

Store cookies in an airtight jar or tin at room temperature for up to three days.

These cookies are sure to become lunch-box favorites. Full of great cocoa flavor, plenty of peanut butter, and nuggets of melted chips, these goodies are crispy on the edges and pillow-soft in the center.

Chocolate Peanut Butter Cookies

½ cup (1 stick) unsalted butter, at room temperature

½ cup chunky peanut butter

1 cup packed dark brown sugar

1 large egg

1 teaspoon vanilla extract

1 cup all-purpose flour

¼ cup unsweetened cocoa powder

½ teaspoon baking soda

½ cup semisweet chocolate chips

1   Heat oven to 350°F.

2   In a mixing bowl, cream butter, peanut butter, and brown sugar until fluffy and smooth. Add egg and vanilla and blend.

3   In a separate bowl, mix flour, cocoa powder, and baking soda. Add to creamed mixture. Stir in chocolate chips.

4   Using either an individual ¼-cup measure or a 2-ounce ice-cream scoop, scoop level amounts of dough and drop 2 inches apart onto greased or nonstick cookie sheets.

5   Bake until cookies are firm to the touch, about 18 minutes. Remove cookies from oven and let them set for 2 minutes. Using a spatula, transfer cookies to a rack and let cool.

Makes about 11 cookies.

To prevent hardening, wrap each cookie individually in plastic wrap and store at room temperature for up to three days.

For peanut butter lovers only! Forget the calories and indulge yourself. If you don't have extra-chunky peanut butter on hand, you can use creamy and add ½ cup chopped peanuts to the cookie dough.

Chunky Peanut Butter Cookies

½ cup (1 stick) unsalted butter, at room temperature

⅔ cup extra-chunky peanut butter

1 cup packed light brown sugar

2 large eggs

1 cup all-purpose flour

1 cup finely ground old-fashioned oats

1   Heat oven to 350°F.

2   In a mixing bowl, cream butter, peanut butter, and sugar until smooth. Add eggs and blend.

3   Stir flour and ground oats into creamed mixture.

4   Using either an individual ¼-cup measure or a 2-ounce ice-cream scoop, scoop level amounts of dough and drop 2 inches apart onto ungreased cookie sheets.

5   Bake until cookies are golden brown, 18–20 minutes. Using a spatula, transfer cookies to a rack and let cool.

Makes about 12 cookies.

To prevent hardening, wrap each cookie individually in plastic wrap and store at room temperature for up to three days.

Could there be life without chocolate chip cookies? They are still
the single most popular cookie in America. This one truly is classic—
no tricks, just a chewy cookie bursting with chocolate flavor.

Classic Chocolate Chip Cookies

½ cup (1 stick) unsalted butter, at room temperature

½ cup packed dark brown sugar

½ cup granulated sugar

1 large egg

2 tablespoons milk

1 teaspoon vanilla extract

1 cup all-purpose flour

½ cup cake flour

½ teaspoon baking powder

¼ teaspoon salt

1 cup semisweet chocolate chips

½ cup coarsely chopped walnuts

1   Heat oven to 375°F.

2   In a mixing bowl, cream butter and both sugars until smooth. Add the egg, milk, and vanilla and blend.

3   In a separate bowl, mix both flours with the baking powder and salt. Add to the creamed mixture. Stir in the chocolate chips and walnuts.

4   Using either an individual ¼-cup measure or a 2-ounce ice-cream scoop, scoop level amounts of dough and drop 2 inches apart onto greased or nonstick cookie sheets.

5   Bake until cookies are lightly browned and firm to the touch, about 15 minutes. Using a spatula, transfer cookies to a rack and let cool.

Makes about 12 cookies.

To prevent hardening, wrap each cookie individually in plastic wrap and store at room temperature for up to three days.

Almost a candy, these no-bake cookies are quick to make—
and quick to be devoured. All you need is a saucepan, a spoon,
and a hankering for a taste of chocolate paradise.

Coco Loco No-Bake Cookies

1 cup granulated sugar

¼ cup (½ stick) unsalted butter

⅓ cup whipping cream

2 tablespoons unsweetened cocoa powder

½ teaspoon vanilla extract

¼ cup creamy peanut butter

1½ cups quick-cooking oats

½ cup raisins

1   Line a cookie sheet with waxed paper and set aside.

2   In a saucepan, combine sugar, butter, whipping cream, and cocoa powder. Heat and stir until blended and smooth. Bring mixture to a full rolling boil and boil for 1 minute.

3   Remove from heat and stir in vanilla and peanut butter until well blended. Add oats and raisins and keep stirring until mixture is thick.

4   To form each cookie, scoop 1 heaping tablespoon and drop onto the waxed paper. Set cookies aside to cool and harden.

Makes about 18 cookies.

Store cookies in an airtight plastic storage bag at room temperature for up to three days. Do not freeze.

The addition of a surprise ingredient—a hint of
pepper—makes these cookies taste fantastic. And while
they are baking, lovely, spicy aromas will fill the kitchen.

Four-Spice Fantasies

2½ cups all-purpose flour

¾ teaspoon cinnamon, plus ¼ teaspoon for garnish

½ teaspoon allspice

½ teaspoon ground cloves

½ teaspoon white pepper

½ teaspoon baking soda

¼ teaspoon salt

½ cup (1 stick) plus 3 tablespoons unsalted butter, at room
   temperature

⅔ cup granulated sugar

⅓ cup dark corn syrup

1 large egg

1   Heat oven to 375°F.

2   Mix flour, ¾ teaspoon cinnamon, the remaining spices, baking soda, and salt in a bowl. Set aside.

3   In a separate bowl, cream butter and sugar until smooth. Add corn syrup and egg and blend.

4   Add the flour mixture and stir to form stiff dough.

5   Roll into 1½-inch balls and drop onto ungreased cookie sheets, spacing 2½ inches apart. Sprinkle tops with the cinnamon reserved for garnish.

6   Bake until just barely firm, about 13 minutes. (Do not overbake.) Using a spatula, transfer cookies to a rack and let cool.

Makes about 18 cookies.

To prevent hardening, wrap each cookie individually in plastic wrap and store at room temperature for up to three days.

These buttery delights guarantee satisfaction
for the sweet tooth with a delicate crunch of
nourishing carrot in every bite.

Fresh Carrot Munchies

¾ cup (1½ sticks) unsalted butter, at room temperature

¾ cup granulated sugar

1 cup shredded raw carrot

½ cup sweetened shredded coconut

Grated rind of 1 lemon (about 1 teaspoon)

2 cups all-purpose flour

1 teaspoon baking powder

½ teaspoon salt

1   Heat oven to 375°F.

2   In a mixing bowl, cream butter and sugar until fluffy and smooth. Add carrot, coconut, and lemon rind and blend.

3   In a separate bowl, mix flour, baking powder, and salt. Add to creamed mixture.

4   Using either an individual ¼-cup measure or a 2-ounce ice-cream scoop, scoop level measures of dough and drop 3 inches apart onto ungreased cookie sheets.

5   Bake until cookies are lightly golden and firm to the touch, 15–18 minutes. Using a spatula, transfer cookies to a rack and let cool.

Makes about 12 cookies.

Store cookies in an airtight jar or tin at room temperature for up to three days.

This delicious licorice-flavored treat has a slightly domed top—perfect for covering with buttery sweet frosting. The cookie's outer crispness yields to a soft, melt-in-your-mouth interior. This dough may be used immediately or covered with plastic wrap and set aside at room temperature for up to four hours. Do not freeze.

Frosted Anise Cookies

3 large eggs

1 cup granulated sugar

¼ cup (½ stick) unsalted butter, melted

1½ teaspoons anise seed

½ teaspoon anise extract

2 cups all-purpose flour

1 teaspoon baking powder

½ teaspoon salt

Anise Butter Frosting (recipe follows)

1   Heat oven to 375°F.

2   In a mixing bowl, beat together eggs and sugar until smooth. Add melted butter, anise seed, and anise extract and blend.

3   In a separate bowl, mix flour, baking powder, and salt. Add to the creamed mixture and stir until batter stiffens into a dough.

4   Scoop 2 level tablespoons of dough and roll to form each cookie. Drop dough onto greased or nonstick cookie sheets, spacing the cookies 2 inches apart.

5   Bake until cookies are firm to the touch and browned on bottom edges, about 12 minutes. Using a spatula, transfer cookies to a rack and let cool.

6   When cookies are completely cool, frost with Anise Butter Frosting.

ANISE BUTTER FROSTING

| ¼ cup (½ stick) unsalted butter, melted |
| 1 teaspoon anise extract |
| 1 cup confectioners' sugar |

1   In a bowl, stir together melted butter and anise extract. Gradually add sugar, mixing until frosting is creamy and spreadable.

2   Immediately frost cooled cookies. Let frosting harden before serving.

Makes about 20 cookies.

Store cookies in an airtight jar or tin at room temperature for up to three days.

Big as a full moon—as seen from earth, that is. This combination of chocolate and graham cracker–flavored cookies sandwiched together with marshmallow cream is sure to be a crowd-pleasing hit. Eat them as a snack or offer them as birthday party treats.

Full Moon Cookies

2 ounces semisweet chocolate, cut into pieces

2 tablespoons whipping cream, half-and-half, or whole milk

1½ cups graham cracker crumbs

⅔ cup all-purpose flour

⅓ cup cake flour

½ teaspoon baking soda

¼ teaspoon salt

½ cup (1 stick) unsalted butter, at room temperature

¾ cup packed light brown sugar

1 large egg

½ teaspoon vanilla extract

1 cup marshmallow cream

1 Place chocolate and whipping cream in the top of a double boiler and melt over barely simmering water. Or, place in a microwavable dish and melt in microwave set on medium power for 1 to 2 minutes. Stir until smooth and set aside.

2   Combine graham cracker crumbs, both flours, baking soda, and salt in a bowl. Set aside.

3   In a separate bowl, cream butter and sugar until smooth. Add egg and vanilla and blend. Add chocolate mixture and blend again. Stir in the graham cracker–flour mixture. Cover dough with plastic wrap and refrigerate for at least 1 hour.

4   Heat oven to 350°F.

5   Scoop 2 level tablespoons of dough and roll to form each cookie. Drop dough onto ungreased cookie sheets, spacing 2½ inches apart. Flatten tops slightly.

6   Bake until tops of cookies look crackled, about 15 minutes. (Cookies will still feel soft in the center.) Remove cookies from oven and let them set for 2 minutes. Using a spatula, transfer cookies to a rack and let cool.

7   After cookies have cooled, center 1 tablespoon marshmallow cream on the flat side of half the cookies. Cover marshmallow filling with the flat side of the remaining cookies and press to sandwich them together.

Makes about 9 sandwich cookies.

To prevent hardening, wrap each sandwich cookie individually in plastic wrap and store at room temperature for up to three days.

The word *cookie* comes from the Dutch word *koekje*, which means "little cake." These soft, tender cookies justify the original definition, and the tasty orange glaze accentuates the citrus flavor. Do not freeze this dough.

Glazed Yogurt Orange Cookies

1 cup (2 sticks) unsalted butter, at room temperature
1½ cups granulated sugar
1 cup plain low-fat yogurt
Grated rind of 2 oranges (about 2 tablespoons)
1 teaspoon orange extract
3 cups all-purpose flour
1 teaspoon baking soda
½ teaspoon salt
Orange Glaze (recipe follows)

1   Heat oven to 375°F.

2   In a mixing bowl, cream butter and sugar until smooth. Add yogurt, orange rind, and orange extract and blend.

3   In a separate bowl, mix flour, baking soda, and salt. Add to the creamed mixture.

4   Using either an individual ¼-cup measure or a 2-ounce ice-cream scoop, scoop level amounts of dough and drop 2½ inches apart onto ungreased cookie sheets.

5   Bake until cookies are lightly golden and feel firm to the touch, about 15 minutes. Using a spatula, transfer cookies to a rack and let cool.

6   When cookies are completely cool, brush with Orange Glaze.

ORANGE GLAZE	Juice of 2 freshly squeezed oranges (about ½ cup)
	¼ cup granulated sugar
	2 teaspoons cornstarch

1   In a small saucepan, mix juice, sugar, and cornstarch. Over low heat, slowly bring to a boil, stirring, until mixture has thickened.

2   Remove from heat and let cool until warm. Brush warm glaze over completely cooled cookies.

Makes about 20 cookies.

Store cookies in a loosely covered container at room temperature for up to three days.

What's good for breakfast can be great as dessert. These terrific-tasting granola cookies are made with maple yogurt to give them a slight caramel flavor. It's perfect for tucking inside a school lunch box next to an apple.

Great Granola Cookies

1 cup coarsely chopped walnuts

1½ cups natural granola cereal (see Note)

1 cup dried tart cherries or cranberries

½ cup (1 stick) unsalted butter, at room temperature

¾ cup packed light brown sugar

1 large egg

¼ cup maple-flavored yogurt

1 teaspoon vanilla extract

1 cup all-purpose flour

½ teaspoon baking soda

½ teaspoon salt

NOTE: Natural granola is sweetened with fruit juice instead of sugar and has no added fat.

1   Heat oven to 375°F.

2   Toast walnuts on a cookie sheet in oven until lightly browned, about 10 minutes. Combine walnuts with granola and cherries in a bowl and set aside.

3   In a mixing bowl, cream butter and sugar until fluffy and smooth. Add egg. Add yogurt and vanilla and blend.

4   In a separate bowl, mix flour, baking soda, and salt. Add to creamed mixture.

5   Using either an individual ¼-cup measure or a 2-ounce ice-cream scoop, scoop level amounts of dough and drop 2 inches apart onto ungreased cookie sheets.

6   Bake until cookies are golden brown, about 15 minutes. Using a spatula, transfer cookies to a rack and let cool.

Makes about 20 cookies.

To prevent hardening, wrap each cookie individually in plastic wrap and store at room temperature for up to three days.

These iced cookies taste better than cake—and are much easier to do. Try them paired with fresh berries or fruit sorbet for an easy yet elegant dessert.

Lemon Poppy Seed Cookies with Lemon Icing

½ cup (1 stick) unsalted butter, at room temperature

1 cup granulated sugar

2 large egg yolks

1 teaspoon vanilla extract

2 teaspoons grated lemon rind (about 2 lemons)

2 tablespoons poppy seeds

½ cup sour cream

2 cups all-purpose flour

2 teaspoons baking powder

½ teaspoon baking soda

¼ teaspoon salt

Lemon Icing (recipe follows)

1. Heat oven to 350°F.

2. In a mixing bowl, cream butter and sugar until smooth. Add egg yolks; then add vanilla and blend. Add lemon rind, poppy seeds, and sour cream.

3. In a separate bowl, mix flour, baking powder, baking soda, and salt. Add to creamed mixture. (Dough will be sticky.)

4. Scoop 2 level tablespoons of dough and roll to form each cookie. Drop onto ungreased cookie sheets, spacing 2 inches apart.

5. Bake until cookies are lightly browned, about 18 minutes. Using a spatula, transfer cookies to a rack and let cool.

6. When cookies have cooled completely, drizzle tops with Lemon Icing.

LEMON ICING

1 cup confectioners' sugar
1 tablespoon butter, at room temperature
2 tablespoons freshly squeezed lemon juice (½ lemon)

1. Place sugar in a bowl. Whisk in butter and lemon juice until smooth.

2. Drizzle icing over tops of cooled cookies. Let icing harden before serving.

Makes about 20 cookies.

Store cookies in an airtight jar or tin at room temperature for up to three days.

In this cookie, sweet and creamy white chocolate blissfully mingles with bitter dark chocolate. The big chunks provide maximum chocolate pleasure.

Light and Dark Chocolate Chunk Cookies

¾ cup (1½ sticks) unsalted butter, at room temperature

¾ cup packed light brown sugar

2 large eggs

½ teaspoon almond extract

2¼ cups all-purpose flour

1 teaspoon baking soda

½ teaspoon salt

1 cup sweetened shredded coconut

6 ounces white chocolate, cut into ½-inch chunks

6 ounces bittersweet chocolate, cut into ½-inch chunks

1   Heat oven to 350°F.

2   In a mixing bowl, cream butter and sugar until smooth. Add eggs and almond extract and blend.

3   In a separate bowl, mix flour, baking soda, and salt and add to the creamed mixture. Stir in coconut and both kinds of chocolate chunks.

4   Using either an individual ¼-cup measure or a 2-ounce ice-cream scoop, scoop level amounts of dough and drop 2 inches apart onto ungreased cookie sheets.

5   Bake until cookies are lightly golden brown, about 15 minutes. Using a spatula, transfer cookies to a rack and let cool.

Makes about 18 cookies.

To prevent hardening, wrap each cookie individually in plastic wrap and store at room temperature for up to three days.

Nutty and oh, so sweet, this delicate,
chewy confection is the perfect
companion to vanilla bean ice cream.

Macadamia Nut Macaroons

1 3½-ounce jar macadamia nuts

½ cup granulated sugar

2 large egg whites

⅔ cup confectioners' sugar

½ cup cake flour

1 Heat oven to 325°F.

2 In a food processor or food grinder, grind the nuts with the granulated sugar until fine. Set aside.

3 Using an electric mixer, beat egg whites in a bowl until thickened. Add confectioners' sugar and beat until shiny. Stir in the nut mixture and flour. Set dough aside for 15 minutes until firm.

4 To form each cookie, scoop 1 rounded tablespoon of dough and drop onto a greased and floured cookie sheet, spacing 3 inches apart.

5 Bake until cookies are lightly golden, about 12 minutes. Remove cookies from oven and let them set for 2 minutes. Using a spatula, carefully transfer cookies to a rack and let cool.

Makes about 16 cookies.

Store cookies in an airtight plastic storage bag at room temperature for up to five days. Do not freeze.

Those who like cinnamon sprinkled on their oatmeal
in the morning will love these cookies. In fact, try one
for a breakfast treat when you need to grab and go.

Oatmeal Cinnamon Cookies

2 cups old-fashioned oats

1½ cups all-purpose flour

1½ teaspoons cinnamon

½ teaspoon baking soda

½ teaspoon salt

1 large egg

1 cup granulated sugar

1 cup (2 sticks) unsalted butter, melted and cooled

1 tablespoon dark molasses

¼ cup milk

½ cup chopped pecans

1   Heat oven to 350°F.

2   Combine oats, flour, cinnamon, baking soda, and salt in a bowl. Set aside.

3   In a separate bowl, beat together egg and sugar. Add butter and continue beating. When completely blended, add molasses and milk and blend again. Stir in the oat mixture and the pecans.

4   Using either an individual ¼-cup measure or a 2-ounce ice-cream scoop, scoop level amounts of dough and drop 2½ inches apart onto ungreased cookie sheets.

5   Bake until cookies are golden brown, about 15 minutes. (Do not overbake.) Remove cookies from oven and let them set for 1 minute. Using a spatula, transfer cookies to a rack and let cool.

Makes about 14 cookies.

To prevent hardening, wrap each cookie individually in plastic wrap and store at room temperature for up to three days.

Sweet, crunchy coconut combined with
seductive, rich white chocolate guarantees
this oatmeal cookie's success.

Oatmeal Coconut White Chocolate Cookies

1 cup (2 sticks) unsalted butter, at room temperature

1 cup packed dark brown sugar

1 large egg

¼ cup whole milk

1 teaspoon almond extract

2 cups all-purpose flour

2 cups old-fashioned oats

1 teaspoon baking soda

½ teaspoon salt

1 cup sweetened shredded coconut

6 ounces white chocolate, cut into ½-inch chunks

1   Heat oven to 350°F.

2   In a mixing bowl, cream butter and sugar until fluffy and smooth. Add egg, milk, and almond extract and blend.

3   In a separate bowl, mix flour, oats, baking soda, and salt. Add to the creamed mixture. Stir in coconut and white chocolate.

4   Using either an individual ¼-cup measure or a 2-ounce ice-cream scoop, scoop level amounts of dough and drop 2 inches apart onto ungreased cookie sheets.

5   Bake until cookies are golden brown, about 15 minutes. Using a spatula, transfer cookies to a rack and let cool.

Makes about 18 cookies.

To prevent hardening, wrap each cookie individually in plastic wrap and store at room temperature for up to three days.

Turn back the clock to the childhood
pleasure and comfort of a cozy kitchen
snack with this big, tasty treat.

Oatmeal Walnut Raisin Cookies

1½ cups old-fashioned oats

1 cup all-purpose flour

½ teaspoon baking soda

½ teaspoon baking powder

½ teaspoon salt

½ cup (1 stick) plus 3 tablespoons unsalted butter, at room
temperature

½ cup packed dark brown sugar

½ cup granulated sugar

1 large egg

1 tablespoon milk

1 teaspoon vanilla extract

1 cup coarsely chopped walnuts

1 cup raisins

1   Heat oven to 350°F.

2   Combine oats, flour, baking soda, baking powder, and salt in a bowl. Set aside.

3   In a separate bowl, cream butter and both sugars until fluffy and smooth. Add egg, milk, and vanilla and blend until smooth. Stir in the oat mixture, walnuts, and raisins.

4   Using either an individual ¼-cup measure or a 2-ounce ice-cream scoop, scoop level amounts of dough and drop 3 inches apart onto ungreased cookie sheets.

5   Bake until edges of cookies are golden brown, about 15 minutes. (Do not overbake.) Remove cookies from oven and let them set for 1 minute. Using a spatula, transfer cookies to a rack and let cool.

Makes about 14 cookies.

To prevent hardening, wrap each cookie individually in plastic wrap and store at room temperature for up to three days.

In the days when homemakers churned cream into butter, cookies such as these served as inspiration for the laborious task. Use colored candy sprinkles to dress them up, or enjoy them unadorned and fresh from the oven.

Old-Fashioned Cream Cookies

1½ cups all-purpose flour

½ cup cake flour

½ teaspoon baking soda

¼ teaspoon salt

¼ teaspoon mace

2 large eggs

1 cup granulated sugar

½ cup whipping cream

⅓ cup (5⅓ tablespoons) unsalted butter, melted and cooled

½ teaspoon vanilla extract

Colored sprinkles

1   Heat oven to 350°F.

2   Combine both flours along with the baking soda, salt, and mace in a bowl. Set aside.

3   In a separate bowl, beat together eggs and sugar until smooth. Add whipping cream, butter, and vanilla and blend. Stir in the flour mixture.

4   Scoop 2 rounded tablespoons of dough and roll to form each cookie. Drop dough onto greased or nonstick cookie sheets, spacing 2 inches apart. Decorate tops with colored sprinkles.

5   Bake until cookies are lightly golden and firm to the touch, about 12 minutes. Using a spatula, transfer cookies to a rack and let cool.

Makes about 18 cookies.

Store cookies in an airtight jar or tin at room temperature for up to three days.

A moist, tasty anytime snack packed with a
one-two punch of fruit and nuts, these cookies
are almost too good to be true.

Plum and Then Some

2 cups all-purpose flour

1 teaspoon cinnamon

½ teaspoon baking soda

¼ teaspoon ground cloves

¼ teaspoon salt

½ cup (1 stick) unsalted butter, at room temperature

1 cup packed light brown sugar

1 large egg

¼ cup orange juice

1 cup chopped pitted dried plums

1 cup chopped walnuts

½ cup chopped dried apricots

½ cup raisins

1   Heat oven to 350°F.

2   Combine flour, cinnamon, baking soda, cloves, and salt in a bowl. Set aside.

3   In a mixing bowl, cream butter and sugar until fluffy and smooth. Add egg and orange juice and blend. Stir in flour mixture and then dried plums, walnuts, apricots, and raisins.

4   Using either an individual ¼-cup measure or a 2-ounce ice-cream scoop, scoop level amounts of dough and drop 2½ inches apart onto ungreased cookie sheets. Flatten each to ½ inch thick.

5   Bake until cookies are golden brown, about 15 minutes. Using a spatula, transfer cookies to a rack and let cool.

Makes about 16 cookies

Store cookies in an airtight plastic storage bag at room temperature for up to three days.

Laced with sweet, syrupy honey, these cookies
are the perfect down-home treat to serve
when family or friends come to visit.

Poppy Seed Honey Cookies

1 cup honey

½ cup (1 stick) unsalted butter

1 teaspoon baking soda

2 large eggs

2½ cups all-purpose flour

½ teaspoon salt

1½ tablespoons poppy seeds

1   In a medium saucepan, combine honey and butter. Bring to a full rolling boil and cook for 1 minute. Remove from heat and stir in baking soda. (Mixture will foam and increase sizably in volume.) Set aside to cool until barely warm.

2   Heat oven to 350°F.

3   Beat eggs into honey mixture; then stir in flour, salt, and poppy seeds. Stir until dough is very stiff.

4   For each cookie, scoop 1 heaping tablespoon of dough and drop onto greased or nonstick cookie sheets, spacing 2½ inches apart.

5   Bake until cookies are firm to the touch, about 10 minutes. (Do not overbake.) Using a spatula, transfer cookies to a rack and let cool.

Makes about 25 cookies.

Store cookies in an airtight jar or tin at room temperature for up to five days. Do not freeze.

Variations on recipes for hermits have
been passed around for years. The best of them
include sour cream as this recipe does.

Sour Cream Hermits

½ cup (1 stick) unsalted butter, at room temperature

1 cup packed dark brown sugar

½ cup sour cream

1 large egg

1½ cups all-purpose flour

1 teaspoon cinnamon

½ teaspoon allspice

½ teaspoon baking soda

¼ teaspoon salt

1 cup chopped pitted dates (see Note)

1 cup chopped walnuts (see Note)

NOTE: **You may substitute raisins and pecans for the dates and walnuts, if desired.**

1   Heat oven to 350°F.

2   In a mixing bowl, cream butter and brown sugar until smooth. Add sour cream and egg and blend.

3   In a separate bowl, mix flour, spices, baking soda, and salt. Add to the creamed mixture. Stir in dates and walnuts.

4   Scoop 2 rounded tablespoons of dough and roll to form each cookie. Drop dough onto greased or nonstick cookie sheets, spacing 2½ inches apart.

5   Bake until cookies are firm to the touch, about 15 minutes. Using a spatula, transfer cookies to a rack and let cool.

Makes about 18 cookies.

Store cookies in an airtight jar or tin at room temperature for up to three days.

Visitors to Charleston, South Carolina, or Savannah, Georgia, have no doubt seen and probably tasted the thin benne seed wafers that are made there. The benne plant, grown in the region, is a sesame plant that produces edible seeds. For the cookies, sesame seeds are toasted first to bring out a nutty, buttery quality that tastes a little like caramel candy. These cookies are a chewier version than is typical of the wafers found in the South.

Southern Sesame Seed Cookies

¼ cup sesame seeds

6 tablespoons (¾ stick) unsalted butter, at room temperature

¾ cup packed dark brown sugar

1 large egg

½ teaspoon vanilla extract

¾ cup all-purpose flour

⅛ teaspoon baking powder

⅛ teaspoon salt

1 Heat oven to 350°F.

2 Toast sesame seeds in a dry skillet over medium-low heat, stirring, until golden brown, about 5 minutes. Set aside to cool.

3 In a mixing bowl, cream butter and brown sugar until smooth. Add egg and vanilla and blend.

4 In a separate bowl, mix flour, toasted sesame seeds, baking powder, and salt. Add to creamed mixture.

5 Scoop 1 rounded tablespoon of dough and drop onto lightly greased or nonstick cookie sheets, spacing 2 inches apart.

6 Bake until cookies are browned on the edges and feel firm to the touch, about 10 minutes. (Do not overbake.) Using a spatula, transfer cookies to a rack and let cool.

Makes about 20 cookies.

Store cookies in an airtight jar or tin at room temperature for up to three days.

The distinctive signature of snickerdoodles is that they are always rolled or dredged in cinnamon sugar before baking. Instead of baking powder, this recipe uses the old-fashioned combination of cream of tartar and baking soda, typical of older-style cake and cookie recipes. This is my rendition of a midwestern Amish recipe my mother found.

Super-Duper Snickerdoodles

½ cup (1 stick) unsalted butter, at room temperature

¾ cup granulated sugar, plus 2 tablespoons

1 large egg

1 tablespoon milk

½ teaspoon vanilla extract

1½ cups all-purpose flour

½ teaspoon cream of tartar

¼ teaspoon baking soda

¼ teaspoon salt

1 tablespoon cinnamon

1   In a mixing bowl, cream butter and ¾ cup granulated sugar until smooth. Add egg, milk, and vanilla and blend.

2   In a separate bowl, mix flour, cream of tartar, baking soda, and salt. Add to the creamed mixture. Cover bowl with plastic wrap and refrigerate for at least 1 hour until dough is firm enough to handle.

3   Heat oven to 375°F.

4   On a plate, mix 2 tablespoons of sugar with cinnamon. Scoop and roll the dough into 1½-inch balls; then roll in cinnamon sugar to coat all sides. Arrange sugar-coated balls on ungreased cookie sheets, spacing 2½ inches apart.

5   Bake until edges of cookies are firm to the touch, about 12 minutes. (Do not overbake.) Using a spatula, transfer cookies to a rack and let cool.

Makes about 14 cookies.

Store cookies in an airtight plastic storage bag at room temperature for up to three days.

Nothing is better to shake off a winter chill than a plateful of these soft, smooth-as-silk cookies and mugs of steaming hot cocoa. This dough may be used immediately or covered with plastic wrap and refrigerated for up to three days. Do not freeze.

Sweet Chocolate Chestnut Smoothies

1 cup (2 sticks) unsalted butter, at room temperature

1 cup unsweetened chestnut puree (see Note)

2 cups granulated sugar

2 large eggs

2 teaspoons vanilla extract

2 cups all-purpose flour

1 teaspoon baking powder

1 teaspoon baking soda

½ teaspoon salt

8 ounces semisweet chocolate or real chocolate chips

Note: Unsweetened chestnut puree is available in the specialty-food sections of most supermarkets.

1 Heat oven to 375°F.

2 In a mixing bowl, cream butter, chestnut puree, and sugar until smooth. Add eggs and vanilla and mix until blended.

3 In a separate bowl, mix flour, baking powder, baking soda, and salt. Add to the creamed mixture.

4 Using either an individual ¼-cup measure or a 2-ounce ice-cream scoop, scoop level amounts of dough and drop 2½ inches apart onto greased or nonstick cookie sheets.

5 Bake until edges of cookies have browned, about 15 minutes. Using a spatula, transfer cookies to a rack and let cool.

6 While cookies are cooling, finely chop the chocolate, place into a small zipper-top plastic storage bag, and seal top. Set bag into a bowl of hot tap water, with sealed top hanging over the bowl's edge, out of the water. When chocolate has completely melted, remove bag from water.

7 Snip a small hole in one corner of the bag. Squeeze out chocolate, drizzling it decoratively over cooled cookies.

Makes about 20 cookies.

Store cookies in a loosely covered container at room temperature for up to three days.

Plenty of texture and sweetness can be
found in these cookies. They are a good
accompaniment to baked apples or poached pears.

Tart Cherry Raisin Cookies

½ cup (1 stick) unsalted butter, at room temperature

¾ cup granulated sugar

½ cup sour cream

½ teaspoon almond extract

1½ cups all-purpose flour

½ teaspoon baking soda

¼ teaspoon salt

¾ cup raisins

¾ cup dried tart cherries (see Note)

NOTE: **You may substitute dried cranberries for the cherries, if desired.**

1   Heat oven to 375°F.

2   In a mixing bowl, cream butter and sugar until smooth. Add sour cream and almond extract and blend.

3   In a separate bowl, mix flour, baking soda, and salt. Add to the creamed mixture. Stir in raisins and cherries.

4   Using either an individual ¼-cup measure or a 2-ounce ice-cream scoop, scoop level amounts of dough and drop 2 inches apart onto ungreased cookie sheets.

5   Bake until cookies are lightly golden brown, 15–17 minutes. Using a spatula, transfer cookies to a rack and let cool.

Makes about 12 cookies.

Store cookies in an airtight jar or tin at room temperature for up to three days.

Sturdy in structure but with a tender crumb, these
sandwiches, with their creamy vanilla-frosting centers,
are yummy and buttery. A great after-school snack.

Vanilla Cream Sandwich Cookies

1¼ cups (2½ sticks) unsalted butter, at room temperature

⅔ cup packed light brown sugar

1 large egg yolk

2 tablespoons vanilla extract

2 cups all-purpose flour

2 cups confectioners' sugar

¼ cup whipping cream

1 Heat oven to 325°F.

2 In a mixing bowl, cream 1 cup (2 sticks) of butter and sugar until fluffy and smooth. Add egg yolk and 1 tablespoon of vanilla and blend.

3 Stir in flour.

4 To form each cookie, roll 1 level tablespoon of dough into a ball and place on ungreased cookie sheets, spacing 2 inches apart. Use a flat-bottomed cup dipped into flour to flatten each cookie into 2½-inch rounds

5 Bake until cookies are set but not browned, about 12 minutes. (Do not overbake.) Remove cookies from oven and let them set for 1 minute. Using a spatula, transfer cookies to a rack and let cool.

6 Prepare frosting while cookies are baking. In a bowl, mix together confectioners' sugar, ¼ cup (½ stick) of butter, whipping cream, and the remaining tablespoon of vanilla until smooth. Consistency should be thick but spreadable.

7 When cookies are completely cool, spread 2 rounded teaspoonfuls of frosting on the underside of half the cookies. Cover filling with the underside of the remaining cookies, pressing to sandwich them together.

Makes about 16 sandwich cookies.

Store cookies in an airtight plastic storage bag at room temperature for up to three days.

2

Shaped

COOKIES

Buttermilk is the secret ingredient that gives this treat
its special taste and tender crumb. A double-layered
cookie surrounds a central dollop of fruit filling. Delicious!

Apricot Pillows

½ cup (1 stick) unsalted butter, at room temperature

1 cup granulated sugar

1 large egg

1 teaspoon vanilla extract

3 cups all-purpose flour

1 teaspoon baking powder

½ teaspoon baking soda

¼ teaspoon salt

½ cup buttermilk

1 cup apricot spreadable fruit

1 Heat oven to 375°F.

2 In a mixing bowl, cream butter and sugar until fluffy and smooth. Add
egg and vanilla and blend.

3   In a separate bowl, mix flour, baking powder, baking soda, and salt. Add the flour mixture to the creamed mixture, alternating with buttermilk to form dough.

4   Turn out half the dough onto a lightly floured surface and roll into a 12-inch round. Using a 3-inch-round cookie cutter, cut out an even number of rounds. Using a 1-inch round cutter, punch out the centers of half of the rounds.

5   Arrange the uncut rounds on ungreased cookie sheets, spacing them 1 inch apart. Moisten the outer edges with a bit of water, then layer the cut-out rounds on top. Center a rounded teaspoon of apricot fruit in the middle hole of each.

6   Bake until cookies are lightly golden around bottom edges and firm to the touch, about 10 minutes. Using a spatula, transfer cookies to a rack and let cool.

7   Repeat with remaining dough, rerolling any scraps.

Makes about 20 cookies.

Store cookies in an airtight jar or tin at room temperature for up to five days.

Bakes like a scone, looks like a scone, tastes like a
cookie. Serve them with fruit and yogurt for a delightful
breakfast treat, midday snack, or even weeknight dessert.

Breakfast Blueberry Scone Cookies

1½ cups all-purpose flour

⅓ cup granulated sugar

1 teaspoon baking powder

¼ teaspoon salt

¼ cup (½ stick) cold unsalted butter, cut into pieces

¾ cup dried blueberries

½ cup buttermilk

1 large egg

Cinnamon sugar, for garnish

1   Heat oven to 375°F.

2   Combine flour, sugar, baking powder, and salt in a bowl. Cut in butter until mixture is crumbly. Stir in blueberries.

3   Mix buttermilk and egg; then add to flour mixture to form dough. (Do not overwork dough.)

4   Turn out dough onto a lightly floured surface and pat out to ¾-inch thickness. Using a 2½-inch round cookie cutter, cut dough into rounds. Push scraps together and cut to use all the dough. Arrange rounds on a nonstick or greased cookie sheet, spacing them 1 inch apart. Sprinkle tops with cinnamon-sugar.

5   Bake until scone cookies are lightly golden and firm to the touch, about 20 minutes. Using a spatula, transfer to a rack to cool.

Makes about 9 scone cookies.

Serve scone cookies while still warm or at room temperature the same day they are baked. For longer storage, freeze in plastic storage bag for up to three months. Defrost at room temperature.

Here, a chocolaty shortbread crust envelops a
luscious peanut butter filling that doubles the
eating pleasure. These cookies are baked in minimuffin tins.

Chocolate Peanut Butter Cups

½ cup (1 stick) plus 2 tablespoons unsalted butter, at room
   temperature

½ cup confectioners' sugar

¼ cup Dutch-processed cocoa powder

1 cup all-purpose flour

¼ cup creamy or chunky peanut butter

½ cup packed light brown sugar

1 large egg

½ teaspoon vanilla extract

1   Heat oven to 350°F.

2   In a mixing bowl, cream ½ cup (1 stick) of butter with confectioners'
    sugar until smooth. Add cocoa, then ¾ cup of flour and mix to form a
    soft dough.

3   Using fingertips, press 2 level teaspoons of dough into each minimuffin
    cup to fill bottom and three-quarters up the sides. (Prepare in two
    batches if using one 12-cup minimuffin tin.)

4   In a mixing bowl, cream the remaining 2 tablespoons of butter, peanut
    butter, and light brown sugar until smooth. Add egg and vanilla and
    blend. Mix in the remaining ¼ cup flour until well blended. Fill
    chocolate cups with peanut butter filling.

5   Bake until filling is golden and set, about 15 minutes. Place minimuffin
    tin on a rack and let cookies cool in the pan 10 minutes. Using a small,
    sharp knife, loosen one edge of each crust from cup sides to lift cookies
    out. Cool completely on rack.

Makes about 24 cookies.

Store cookies in an airtight plastic storage bag at room temperature for
up to three days.

One taste of these tender cookies and you'll find it difficult
to stop. Since they are not very sweet, try pairing them
with fruit sorbet for a delicious dessert or snack.

Creamed Shortbread Cookies

½ cup (1 stick) unsalted butter, at room temperature

¼ cup confectioners' sugar

¼ cup sour cream

1¼ cups cake flour

¼ teaspoon baking soda

¼ teaspoon salt

1 Heat oven to 350°F.

2 In a mixing bowl, cream butter and sugar until smooth. Add sour cream and blend.

3 In a separate bowl, mix flour, baking soda, and salt and add to creamed mixture.

4 Turn out dough onto a lightly floured surface and roll to ¼-inch thickness. Using a 2½-inch round cookie cutter, cut rounds of dough. Reroll scraps and cut to use all the dough. Arrange cookies on ungreased cookie sheets, spacing them 1 inch apart. Prick cookie tops with a fork in several places.

5 Bake until cookies are lightly golden, about 15 minutes. (Do not overbake.) Using a spatula, transfer cookies to a rack and let cool.

Makes about 12 cookies.

Store cookies in an airtight jar or tin at room temperature for up to three days.

These addicting cookies deliver triple
pleasure with the tantalizing tastes of
dates, tangy citrus, and bits of pecan.

Date Nut Sweeties

½ cup (1 stick) unsalted butter, at room temperature

¾ cup granulated sugar

¼ cup sour cream

1½ cups all-purpose flour

½ teaspoon baking soda

½ teaspoon salt

1 8-ounce package pitted dates

Grated rind of 1 orange (about 1 tablespoon)

½ cup chopped pecans

1   In a mixing bowl, cream butter and ½ cup of sugar until smooth. Add sour cream and blend.

2   In a separate bowl, mix flour, baking soda, and salt. Add to creamed mixture. Cover with plastic wrap and refrigerate for at least 1 hour.

3   Chop dates with the remaining ¼ cup sugar and orange rind by hand or in a food processor. Add pecans and continue to chop until mixture has a uniform consistency. Set aside.

4   Heat oven to 375°F.

5   Turn out chilled dough onto a floured surface and roll into a 14″ × 10″ rectangle. Distribute date filling evenly over dough.

6   Beginning with the long side, roll up dough tightly, jelly-roll style. Cut crosswise into 1-inch-thick slices. Arrange each slice cut side up, and flatten with a spatula to ½-inch thickness. With the spatula, transfer dough slices to ungreased cookie sheets, spacing slices 2 inches apart.

7   Bake until edges of cookies are lightly golden and tops are firm, 10–12 minutes. Remove cookies from oven and let them set for 1 minute. Using a spatula, transfer cookies to a rack to cool.

Makes about 14 cookies.

Store cookies in an airtight jar or tin at room temperature for up to three days.

These are lovely tea cakes, light as air and soft as a cloud. Traditionally, madeleines are baked in special shell-shaped molds. You can, however, successfully bake these in a minimuffin tin instead, using the same amount of batter per cookie as with a madeleine pan. These are particularly good if eaten while still slightly warm.

French Madeleines

1 cup cake flour

½ teaspoon baking powder

¼ teaspoon salt

3 large eggs

⅔ cup granulated sugar

2 teaspoons grated lemon rind

1 teaspoon orange extract (see Note)

¾ cup (1½ sticks) unsalted butter, melted and cooled

¼ cup confectioners' sugar

NOTE: **You may substitute vanilla for the orange extract, if desired.**

1   Heat oven to 350°F.

2   Sift cake flour, baking powder, and salt into a bowl. Set aside.

3   In a separate bowl, use an electric mixer to beat eggs until light in color. Add granulated sugar, lemon rind, and orange extract. Beat on high speed for 2 minutes, until mixture has thickened and volume has slightly increased.

4   Using a rubber spatula, gently stir in the flour mixture, followed by the melted butter, until completely incorporated. (Batter will be light and spongy.)

5   Spoon 1 rounded tablespoon of batter into each greased madeleine mold or minimuffin cup.

6   Bake until cookies are lightly golden and firm to the touch, 10–12 minutes. Immediately invert pan over a cooling rack to unmold cookies.

7   While cookies are warm, sift confectioners' sugar over tops.

Makes about 36 cookies.

Store cookies in an airtight plastic storage bag at room temperature for up to three days. If freezing cookies, omit the dusting of confectioners' sugar.

Kolacky, a pastry beloved in Eastern Europe, has a rich,
tender crust of cream cheese that surrounds a sweet,
jamlike fruit filling. It is the perfect dessert cookie.

Fruit and Cream Cheese Kolackys

½ cup (1 stick) unsalted butter, at room temperature

4 ounces cream cheese, at room temperature

½ cup granulated sugar

1½ cups cake flour

1 cup canned fruit filling or spreadable fruit (prune, cherry, apricot,

or blueberry—see Note)

**NOTE: Fruit fillings are available in ready-to-use 12-ounce cans in most
supermarkets.**

1   In a mixing bowl, cream butter and cream cheese until blended. Add sugar and beat until smooth.

2   Add flour, ½ cup at a time, and mix into a dough. Press dough into a ball, cover with plastic wrap, and refrigerate at least 1 hour.

3   Heat oven to 350°F.

4   Turn out chilled dough onto a lightly floured surface and roll into a 15-inch circle. Using a 3-inch round cookie cutter, cut rounds of dough.

5   Center 1 rounded teaspoon fruit filling onto each dough round. Form open-topped dumplings by lifting up the outside edges of dough to surround, but not cover, the filling. Arrange cookies on ungreased cookie sheets, spacing them 1½ inches apart.

6   Bake until edges of cookies are golden, about 15 minutes. Remove cookies from oven and let them set for 1 minute. Using a spatula, transfer cookies to a rack and let cool.

7   Repeat with remaining dough, rerolling any scraps.

Makes about 25 cookies.

Store cookies in an airtight jar or tin at room temperature for up to three days.

These individual cookie tarts have a buttery,
not overly sweet base and can be filled with
your choice of fruit preserves or jellies.

Jelly Buttons

1 cup (2 sticks) unsalted butter, at room temperature

½ cup granulated sugar

1 large egg

1½ teaspoons vanilla extract

1½ cups all-purpose flour

1 cup cake flour

1 cup fruit preserves or jelly

1   Heat oven to 350°F.

2   In a mixing bowl, cream butter and sugar until fluffy and smooth. Add egg and vanilla and blend.

3   Add both flours and stir to form a stiff dough.

4   Pat dough into a ball then roll out on a lightly floured surface to ¼-inch thickness. Using a 3-inch round cookie cutter, cut rounds of dough. Arrange the rounds on ungreased cookie sheets, spacing 2 inches apart. Using your fingers, raise the outside edges of each round to shape into a tart shell. Fill each center depression with 1 level tablespoon of fruit preserves or jelly.

5   Bake until crust is firm but not browned, about 15 minutes. (Jelly will be soft while hot, but will set firm when cool.) Using a spatula, transfer cookies to a rack and let cool.

6   Reroll remaining dough scraps, and repeat cutting, filling, and baking.

Makes about 14 cookie tarts

Store cookies in an airtight jar or tin at room temperature for up to five days.

These light, spongy cookies are often used to line a mold or provide a base for desserts such as tiramisu, chocolate mousse, fruit pudding, or English trifle. They happen to be pretty tasty on their own, as well.

Luscious Ladyfingers

3 large eggs, separated

½ cup granulated sugar

1 teaspoon grated orange rind

¼ teaspoon cream of tartar

⅔ cup cake flour

¼ cup confectioners' sugar

1   Heat oven to 350°F.

2   In a medium bowl, combine egg yolks and ¼ cup of granulated sugar. Beat until thick and smooth. Add orange rind and stir to combine. Set aside.

3   In another medium bowl, beat egg whites with cream of tartar until thick. Add the remaining ¼ cup granulated sugar and continue to beat until stiff peaks form.

4   Add a third of the whites to the yolk mixture and gently stir to blend. Sift half of the cake flour over the batter. Using a rubber spatula, fold in flour. Add another third of the whites and fold in. Sift remaining cake flour over batter and fold in; fold in remaining whites.

5   Fit a pastry bag with an open round tip and fill with batter. Push batter out onto a greased or nonstick cookie sheet in a controlled line to form cookies 4 inches long and 1½ inches wide. Space cookies 2 inches apart. If possible, use a second greased cookie sheet to bake all the cookies at once. (Batter is delicate and deflates quickly.) Sift confectioners' sugar liberally over the cookies through a small fine-meshed sieve.

6   Bake until cookies are lightly golden, about 10 minutes. Using a spatula, transfer cookies to a rack and let cool.

Makes about 18 cookies.

Store cookies in an airtight plastic storage bag at room temperature for up to three days.

These old-fashioned favorites
guarantee a buttery mouthful of home-
baked goodness with every bite.

Mint-Iced Sugar Cookies

1 cup (2 sticks) unsalted butter, at room temperature

½ cup granulated sugar

2 large eggs

1 teaspoon vanilla extract

2 cups all-purpose flour

Mint Cream Icing (recipe follows)

1 Heat oven to 375°F.

2 In a mixing bowl, cream butter and sugar until smooth. Add eggs and
vanilla and blend.

3 Stir in flour.

4 Fit a pastry bag with an open round tip and fill with cookie dough. Push
dough out of bag onto greased or nonstick cookie sheets, shaping it into

3-inch circles, squares, triangles, or zigzags. Space shapes about 1 inch apart.

5   Bake just until bottom edges of cookies are beginning to brown, about 10 minutes. Using a spatula, transfer cookies to a rack to cool.

6   When cookies have cooled completely, drizzle tops with Mint Cream Icing.

MINT CREAM ICING	1 cup confectioners' sugar
	5–6 tablespoons whipping cream
	1 teaspoon peppermint extract

1   In a bowl, stir together sugar, whipping cream, and peppermint extract until smooth. Use enough cream to obtain an icing that falls heavily and slowly off a spoon.

2   Immediately drizzle icing over tops of cooled cookies. Let icing harden before serving.

Makes about 18 cookies.

Store cookies in an airtight plastic storage bag at room temperature for up to three days.

Deeply flavored and darkly colored with molasses,
these cookies are pure Americana. Sorghum syrup can
be substituted for the molasses (and was, in years past).

Molasses Cookies

2 cups all-purpose flour

¾ teaspoon cinnamon

½ teaspoon ginger

¼ teaspoon nutmeg

½ teaspoon baking soda

½ teaspoon salt

¼ cup (½ stick) unsalted butter, at room temperature

¼ cup granulated sugar, plus 1 tablespoon for garnish

1 large egg

2 tablespoons rum, light or dark

2 tablespoons milk

½ cup dark molasses

1   Combine flour, spices, baking soda, and salt in a bowl. Set aside.

2   In a separate bowl, cream butter and ¼ cup sugar until smooth. Add egg, rum, and milk and blend.

3   Add flour mixture, alternating with molasses until dough is formed. Cover bowl with plastic wrap and refrigerate for at least 1 hour.

4   Heat oven to 375°F.

5   Turn out dough onto a lightly floured surface and roll out to ¼-inch thickness. Using a 2½-inch cookie cutter, cut dough into shapes. Reroll scraps and cut to use all the dough. Arrange dough shapes on a greased or nonstick cookie sheet, spacing them 1 inch apart. Sprinkle tops with the sugar reserved for garnish.

6   Bake until cookies are just firm to the touch, about 10 minutes. (Do not overbake.) Using a spatula, transfer cookies to a rack and let cool.

Makes about 20 cookies.

Store cookies in an airtight plastic storage bag at room temperature for up to three days.

Biscotti is an Italian term for a cookie that is "twice baked." The second trip to the oven is the one that dries and crisps the cookies after they are sliced. True biscotti are dunked into a hot or cold drink as you eat to soften them. Here is a once-baked "nearly" biscotti version made with apricots and almonds that produces tender, chewy cookie slices that are great eating any time of the day or evening.

Nearly Biscotti

½ cup natural, skin-on whole almonds

1¼ cups all-purpose flour

¾ teaspoon baking powder

¼ teaspoon salt

½ teaspoon grated lemon rind

¼ cup (½ stick) unsalted butter, at room temperature

½ cup granulated sugar

1 large egg

¼ cup coarsely chopped dried apricots

1   Heat oven to 350°F. Position oven rack in top third of oven.

2   Toast almonds on cookie sheet in oven for 15 minutes. Let cool and chop coarsely. Reduce oven temperature to 325°F.

3   Sift flour, baking powder, and salt into a bowl. Stir in lemon rind and set aside.

4   In a mixing bowl, cream butter and sugar until smooth. Add egg and blend. Stir in the flour mixture; add toasted almonds and apricots.

5   On a work surface, roll dough into a log, 14 inches long and 2 inches in diameter. Press on the top to flatten log into a ¾-inch-thick loaf. Transfer loaf to a parchment-paper (or nonstick mat) lined 17″ × 12″ baking sheet.

6   Bake until loaf is lightly golden and feels firm to the touch, about 45 minutes. Place baking sheet on a rack for 10 minutes to let loaf cool slightly.

7   Transfer warm loaf to cutting board. Using a serrated bread knife, cut into diagonal slices, ½ inch thick. (Slice while warm to avoid crumbling.) Let cookie slices cool completely on rack.

Makes about 24 cookies.

Store cookies in an airtight jar or tin at room temperature for up to five days.

As these cookies bake, the orange marmalade oozes out of the dough just enough to caramelize the bottoms and glaze the tops. The crust is cheesy—not sweet—and is the perfect foil for the bittersweet marmalade.

Orange Marmalade Cookies

1 cup (2 sticks) unsalted butter, at room temperature

4 ounces cream cheese, at room temperature

1 large egg

2 cups all-purpose flour

1 cup orange marmalade

1   In a mixing bowl, cream butter and cream cheese until well blended. Add egg and blend until smooth.

2   Stir in flour to form a dough. Wrap dough in plastic wrap and refrigerate at least 3 hours.

3   Heat oven to 350°F.

4   Divide chilled dough in half. Working with one-half at a time, turn out onto a floured surface and roll into a 12-inch square. Spread surface of each square of dough evenly with ½ cup of the marmalade.

5   Roll up each square of dough jelly-roll style. Trim and discard uneven ends. Cut crosswise slices, 1 inch thick, and transfer them to greased or nonstick cookie sheets, cut side down and 1 inch apart. (Dough will be very soft and will resemble the petals of an opened flower when placed on the cookie sheet.)

6   Bake until cookies are browned on the bottom and glazed on top, about 15 minutes. Using a spatula, transfer cookies to a rack and let cool.

Makes about 22 cookies.

Store cookies in an airtight jar or tin at room temperature for up to three days.

Thumbprints get their name from the depression made in the center of each round cookie (thumbprint size) that is filled with fruit. This nutty-tasting cookie is baked with a filling of plum butter instead of the usual jam or preserves. Plum butter is prepared with citrus and aromatic spices that provide extra flavor. Substitute another fruit butter, if desired.

Plum Thumbprints

1 cup all-purpose flour

½ cup ground almonds

½ teaspoon grated lemon rind

¼ teaspoon allspice

¼ teaspoon salt

½ cup (1 stick) unsalted butter, at room temperature

⅓ cup granulated sugar, plus 2 tablespoons for garnish

1 large egg

½ teaspoon vanilla extract

¼ cup plum butter

1   Heat oven to 350°F.

2   Combine flour, almonds, lemon rind, allspice, and salt in a bowl. Set
    aside.

3   In a separate bowl, cream butter and ⅓ cup of sugar until smooth. Add
    egg and vanilla and blend. Add the flour mixture and stir to form a soft
    dough.

4   To form each cookie, scoop 1 rounded tablespoon of dough and roll into
    a 1½-inch ball. Pour 2 tablespoons granulated sugar onto a small plate.
    Roll each dough ball into the sugar to coat all sides. Place dough balls on
    greased or nonstick cookie sheets spacing them 2 inches apart. Make a
    depression in the center of each cookie, spreading it to 2 inches in
    diameter. Fill each depression with plum butter, about ½ teaspoon for
    each cookie.

5   Bake until cookie edges feel firm, about 15 minutes. Using a spatula,
    transfer cookies to a rack and let cool.

Makes about 16 cookies.

Store cookies in an airtight plastic storage bag at room temperature for
up to four days.

Creamy and soft with that sweet,
old-fashioned taste, this delightful
cookie will appeal to kids of all ages.

Sour Cream Jumbles

½ cup (1 stick) unsalted butter, at room temperature

1 cup granulated sugar

½ cup sour cream

1 teaspoon vanilla extract

2 cups all-purpose flour

½ teaspoon baking soda

¼ teaspoon salt

¼ teaspoon nutmeg

1   In a mixing bowl, cream butter and sugar until smooth. Add sour cream and vanilla and blend.

2   In a separate bowl, mix flour, baking soda, and salt and add to creamed mixture. Wrap dough in plastic wrap and refrigerate for at least 1 hour.

3   Heat oven to 375°F.

4   Divide chilled dough in half and roll out each half between 2 sheets of waxed paper to a thickness of ¼ inch. Peel off top piece of waxed paper and use a 2½-inch cookie cutter to cut dough into shapes. Reroll and cut any scraps. Repeat with remaining half of dough. Arrange dough shapes on ungreased cookie sheets, spacing them 2 inches apart. Sprinkle tops lightly with nutmeg.

5   Bake until bottom edges of cookies have just begun to brown, about 10 minutes. Using a spatula, transfer cookies to a rack and let cool.

Makes about 26 cookies.

Store cookies in an airtight jar or tin at room temperature for up to three days. Do not freeze dough. Baked cookies may be frozen in plastic storage bags.

Not overly sweet, this cookie has a texture similar
to rich, buttery pastry with a caramel-like toasted-
nut filling. It is terrific served with a cup of hot cocoa.

Toasted–Pine Nut Swirls

1½ cups all-purpose flour

3 tablespoons granulated sugar

1 teaspoon baking powder

¼ teaspoon salt

½ cup (1 stick) cold unsalted butter, cut into pieces

½ cup whipping cream

½ cup pine nuts

⅓ cup packed light brown sugar

1 large egg yolk

1 tablespoon confectioners' sugar, for garnish

1   Combine flour, granulated sugar, baking powder, and salt in a bowl. Cut in butter until mixture is crumbly. Add whipping cream and mix to form dough. Wrap dough in plastic wrap and refrigerate at least 1 hour.

2   Heat oven to 350°F.

3   Toast pine nuts on a cookie sheet in oven until golden brown, 8–10 minutes. Combine toasted pine nuts and light brown sugar in food processor. Pulse to finely chop, then add egg yolk and process until smooth paste forms. Set filling aside.

4   Turn out chilled dough onto a floured surface and roll into a 12″ × 10″ rectangle. Spread pine nut filling evenly over surface of dough.

5   Beginning with the long side, roll up dough tightly, jelly-roll style. Cut crosswise into ¾-inch-thick slices. Arrange each slice, cut side down, on nonstick or parchment-paper-lined cookie sheets, spacing slices 1½ inches apart.

6   Bake until cookies are firm to the touch, about 15 minutes. Using a spatula, transfer cookies to a rack and let cool.

7   While cookies are still warm, sift confectioners' sugar over tops.

Makes about 16 cookies.

Store cookies in an airtight plastic storage bag for up to five days. If freezing cookies, omit the dusting of confectioners' sugar.

3

Bar COOKIES

The success of these easy-to-make bar cookies lies in the exciting contrast of chewy, sweet coconut harmoniously combined with the slightly tart taste of dried cranberries or cherries. A cookie to remember.

Coconut Bars

½ cup all-purpose flour

1 teaspoon cinnamon

¼ teaspoon baking soda

¼ teaspoon salt

½ cup (1 stick) unsalted butter, at room temperature

½ cup packed light brown sugar

1 large egg

1½ cups sweetened shredded coconut

½ cup dried fruit, such as cranberries or tart cherries

1   Heat oven to 350°F.

2   Combine flour, cinnamon, baking soda, and salt in a bowl. Set aside.

3   In a separate bowl, cream butter and sugar until smooth. Add egg and blend. Add flour mixture and blend. Stir in coconut and dried fruit until thoroughly mixed.

4   Spread evenly into an ungreased 8-inch square baking pan.

5   Bake until cookies are firm to the touch and browned, about 20 minutes. Place pan on a rack to cool; cut into 2½″ × 1½″ bars.

Makes about 15 bar cookies.

Store cookies covered in the baking pan at room temperature for up to three days.

A sweet, fruity filling is sandwiched between two layers of nutty cookie crust in this treat. A glass of milk is the ideal companion for this cookie.

Fig Sandwich Fingers

1½ cups all-purpose flour

⅔ cup packed light brown sugar

½ cup (1 stick) plus 2 tablespoons unsalted butter, slightly softened

½ cup finely chopped walnuts

1 cup finely chopped dried figs

1 teaspoon grated lemon rind

¼ cup dark corn syrup

1   Heat oven to 350°F.

2   In a mixing bowl, stir together flour and sugar. Cut in butter until mixture forms coarse crumbs and butter is evenly dispersed. Add walnuts and mix until fine crumbs form. Set aside.

3   In a separate bowl, combine figs and lemon rind. Add corn syrup and stir until thoroughly combined.

4   Spread 1½ cups of the crumb mixture into an ungreased 8-inch square baking pan. Press to pack evenly in pan bottom. Spread fig mixture in an even layer over crumb mixture in pan. Sprinkle remaining crumb mixture over fig layer and press gently to completely enclose the filling.

5   Bake until cookies are golden brown, about 25 minutes. Place pan on a rack to cool; cut into 2½″ × 1¼″ bars.

Makes about 18 bar cookies.

Store cookies covered in the baking pan at room temperature for up to five days. Do not freeze.

Sweet chocolate chips soften into a velvet
topping that prolongs the pleasure of this thick,
chewy brownie. It literally melts in your mouth.

Fudge Melties

4 ounces unsweetened chocolate, cut into pieces

½ cup (1 stick) plus 2 tablespoons unsalted butter, cut into pieces

3 large eggs

1¼ cups granulated sugar

1 tablespoon instant coffee granules

1½ teaspoons vanilla extract

¾ cup all-purpose flour

1 cup semisweet chocolate chips

1   Heat oven to 350°F.

2   Melt chocolate and butter in the top of a double boiler over barely simmering water. Or, place in a microwavable dish and melt in microwave set on medium power for 2½ minutes. Stir until smooth, remove from heat, and set aside to cool.

3   In a mixing bowl, combine eggs, sugar, instant coffee, and vanilla. Beat with an electric mixer on medium speed until mixture is light in color and thick, about 1 minute. Reduce speed to low, add chocolate mixture, and blend.

4   Stir in the flour. Pour batter into a greased 8-inch square baking pan and spread evenly.

5   Bake until center feels firm to the touch, about 25 minutes. Place pan on a rack and immediately sprinkle chocolate chips on cookies, spreading with a thin metal spatula until chocolate has melted into a smooth, even layer. When cool, cut into 2½-inch squares.

Makes about 9 bar cookies.

Store cookies covered in the baking pan at room temperature for up to three days.

Just the mention of German chocolate evokes a warm, nostalgic response in most people. The taste of these brownies will confirm the validity of your craving for an old-fashioned favorite.

German Chocolate Brownies

4 ounces German sweet chocolate, cut into pieces

10 tablespoons unsalted butter

2 large eggs plus 2 egg yolks

½ cup granulated sugar

2½ teaspoons vanilla extract

½ cup cake flour

⅛ teaspoon salt

⅔ cup cream of coconut (see Note)

1 cup sweetened shredded coconut

¾ cup pecan pieces

NOTE: **Cream of coconut is available where drink mixers are located in supermarkets.**

1   Heat oven to 325°F.

2   Combine chocolate pieces with 6 tablespoons of butter in a saucepan. Melt and stir to blend. (Do not try to melt in microwave.)

3   In a mixing bowl, combine 2 eggs and the sugar. Beat until light and fluffy, then add 1½ teaspoons of vanilla. Stir in the melted chocolate mixture, flour, and salt. Pour and spread evenly into a greased 8-inch square baking pan.

4   Bake until firmly set in center, about 30 minutes. Place pan on a rack to cool.

5   Meanwhile, to make the frosting, combine cream of coconut, the remaining 4 tablespoons of butter, 2 egg yolks, and the remaining teaspoon vanilla in a saucepan. Cook and stir over medium heat until thickened and beginning to boil. Remove from heat and immediately stir in coconut and pecans. Transfer to a bowl and set aside to cool.

6   Spread cooled coconut frosting evenly over cooled brownies in pan. Let stand at least 1 hour before cutting into 2½" squares.

Makes about 9 brownies.

Store covered in the baking pan at room temperature for up to three days or in refrigerator for up to five days. Bring back to room temperature to serve.

Key limes, native to Key West, Florida, are smaller in size and more tart in taste than common Persian limes. The juice from these little limes made key lime pie famous. Since most key lime pies have graham cracker crusts, these bar cookies also are made with a graham cracker–enhanced cookie crust and a tangy, key lime curd topping. At least two producers in Key West bottle the juice, so it is available nationwide in most supermarkets these days.

Key Lime Bar Cookies

½ cup (1 stick) plus 6 tablespoons unsalted butter, at room
    temperature

3 tablespoons packed dark brown sugar

1 cup all-purpose flour

⅓ cup graham cracker crumbs

½ cup granulated sugar

⅓ cup key lime juice

3 large egg yolks

1 Heat oven to 350°F.

2 In a mixing bowl, cream ½ cup (1 stick) of butter with brown sugar until smooth.

3 Add flour and graham cracker crumbs, mixing to form dough. Press evenly into bottom of ungreased 8-inch square baking pan.

4 Bake until golden brown, about 20 minutes.

5 Meanwhile, combine the remaining 6 tablespoons butter with granulated sugar, key lime juice, and egg yolks in a saucepan. Cook, whisking constantly, over medium-low heat until mixture thickens, 8–10 minutes. (Do not boil.) Remove from heat and set aside until crust is removed from oven. (Curd will continue to thicken as it cools.)

6 Pour warm lime curd over warm baked crust, tilting pan to distribute topping evenly. Place pan on a rack to cool to room temperature. Loosely cover pan and refrigerate until cold. When cold, cut into 2-inch squares.

Makes about 16 bar cookies.

Store cookies covered in the baking pan in refrigerator for up to five days. Do not freeze.

Home bakers have been serving up these delectable bar cookies
for decades. Their timeless appeal lies in the contrasts of flavor and
texture—a silken, sweet-tart topping over a rich, crumbly crust.

Love Those Lemon Dreams

½ cup (1 stick) unsalted butter, at room temperature

⅓ cup confectioners' sugar, plus 1 tablespoon for garnish

1 cup plus 2 tablespoons all-purpose flour

2 large whole eggs and 1 large egg yolk

¾ cup granulated sugar

3 tablespoons freshly squeezed lemon juice (about 1 lemon)

1   Heat oven to 350°F.

2   In a mixing bowl, cream butter and ⅓ cup confectioners' sugar until smooth.

3   Add 1 cup flour and mix to form a crumbly dough. Spread into an ungreased 8-inch square baking pan and press to pack evenly in the bottom of the pan.

4   Bake until lightly golden, about 15 minutes.

5   Meanwhile, beat whole eggs and yolk in a mixing bowl until foamy. Add granulated sugar and 2 tablespoons flour and beat until thick and smooth. Add lemon juice and blend.

6   When crust is baked, remove from oven and pour lemon topping over the hot crust. Return to oven and bake until topping is set and golden brown, about 15 minutes. Place pan on a rack and let cool; sift 1 tablespoon confectioners' sugar evenly over the top and cut into 2½″ × 2″ bars.

Makes about 12 bar cookies.

Store cookies covered in the baking pan at room temperature for up to two days or in the refrigerator for up to three days. Do not freeze.

Maple-flavored caramel loaded with
walnuts sits atop a divine cream
cheese crust in these cookies.

Maple Walnut Tassies

1 cup (2 sticks) unsalted butter, at room temperature

1 3-ounce package cream cheese, at room temperature

¼ cup confectioners' sugar

1 cup all-purpose flour

¼ cup pure maple syrup

⅔ cup packed light brown sugar

¼ cup whipping cream

1½ cups walnut pieces

1. Heat oven to 350°F.

2. In a mixing bowl, cream ½ cup (1 stick) of butter with cream cheese until smooth. Add confectioners' sugar and blend.

3. Stir in flour and mix to form a crumbly dough. Spread dough in an ungreased 8-inch square baking pan and press dough to pack it into the bottom of the pan.

4. Bake until lightly golden, about 15 minutes.

5. While crust is baking, combine the remaining ½-cup butter with maple syrup in a saucepan. Cook over medium heat until butter melts, then add brown sugar and stir to dissolve. Bring to a rolling boil and continue to boil for 2 minutes. Remove from heat and stir in whipping cream and walnut pieces.

6. When crust is baked, remove from oven and immediately pour maple topping over the hot crust. Return pan to oven and bake until topping is bubbling but center is firm when pan is shaken, about 25 minutes. Place pan on a rack to cool; cut into 2-inch squares.

Makes about 16 bar cookies.

Store cookies covered in the baking pan at room temperature for up to five days.

These are classic and irresistible. A butter-rich crust supports a candy-sweet toffee filling chockfull of pecans. Make these cookie squares for family gatherings or potluck parties.

Pecan Squares

3 cups all-purpose flour

1 teaspoon baking powder

½ teaspoon salt

2 cups (4 sticks) unsalted butter, at room temperature

1 cup granulated sugar

2 large eggs

½ teaspoon vanilla extract

½ cup honey

1¼ cups packed light brown sugar

¼ cup whipping cream

4 cups (about 1 pound) coarsely chopped pecans

1　Combine flour, baking powder, and salt in a bowl. Set aside.

2　In a mixing bowl, cream 1 cup (2 sticks) butter with ¾ cup granulated sugar until smooth. Add eggs, one at a time. Add vanilla and blend.

3   Stir in flour mixture to form dough. Spread dough in a nonstick 15" × 10" × 1" jelly-roll pan and press evenly into the bottom of the pan. Refrigerate dough overnight or freeze until firm, about 30 minutes.

4   Heat oven to 375°F.

5   Bake crust until lightly golden, 12–15 minutes. Remove from oven and place pan on a rack.

6   While crust is baking, combine the remaining 1 cup butter with the honey, light brown sugar, and the remaining ¼ cup granulated sugar in a large saucepan. Cook over medium heat while stirring until mixture comes to a boil. Cook at a boil for 2 minutes. Remove pan from heat and stir in whipping cream and pecans.

7   Pour warm filling over baked crust and return to oven. Bake until topping is bubbling and center is firm when pan is shaken, about 20 minutes. Place pan on a rack and let cool. When completely cool, invert pan over cutting board to release pastry in one piece. Trim ½ inch of the hardened outside edge off each side. Turn pastry pecan-side up to cut cookies into 2¼-inch squares.

Makes about 24 bar cookies.

Store cookies in an airtight plastic storage bag at room temperature for up to five days.

These cookies have a shortbread crust enhanced with
lemon and ginger to complement the raspberry-flavored
filling and crumbly almond topping.

Raspberry Bars

¾ cup (1½ sticks) unsalted butter, at room temperature

⅓ cup confectioners' sugar, plus 1 tablespoon for garnish

½ teaspoon grated lemon rind

¼ teaspoon ginger

1½ cups all-purpose flour

¼ cup finely chopped almonds

2 tablespoons dark brown sugar

¼ teaspoon baking powder

½ cup raspberry spreadable fruit or preserves

1   Heat oven to 350°F.

2   In a mixing bowl, cream ½ cup (1 stick) of butter and ⅓ cup confectioners' sugar until smooth.

3   Add lemon rind, ginger, and 1 cup of the flour. Mix to form a smooth dough. Spread into an ungreased 8-inch square baking pan and press to pack evenly in the bottom.

4   Bake until crust is set but not brown, about 15 minutes. While crust is baking, combine the remaining ½ cup flour with almonds, brown sugar, and baking powder in a bowl and mix together. Add the remaining ¼ cup of butter and stir until mixture is crumbly.

5   When crust is done baking, place pan on rack and spread raspberry fruit onto hot crust using a thin metal spatula.

6   Sprinkle almond–brown sugar topping over fruit filling and press down lightly to form an even layer. Return to oven and bake until topping is golden brown, about 30 minutes. Place pan on a rack and let cool; sift 1 tablespoon confectioners' sugar evenly over the top and cut into 2½″ × 2″ bars.

Makes about 12 bar cookies.

Store cookies covered in the baking pan at room temperature for up to five days.

Cooked rhubarb is sandwiched between an oat and nut streusel crust to make a fruit bar cookie that resembles pie. While the concept is old-fashioned, this cookie never goes out of style.

Rhubarb Oat Bar Cookies

¾ cup all-purpose flour

¾ cup old-fashioned oats

½ cup finely chopped pecans or walnuts

½ cup packed dark brown sugar

¼ teaspoon salt

½ cup (1 stick) unsalted butter, slightly softened

2 cups chopped rhubarb, fresh or frozen

½ cup granulated sugar

1 tablespoon cornstarch

2 tablespoons orange juice

½ teaspoon vanilla extract

1   Heat oven to 350°F.

2   Combine flour, oats, nuts, brown sugar, and salt in a bowl. Add butter in tablespoon-size pieces and stir until mixture is crumbly. Spread half the streusel (1½ cups) in a greased 8-inch square baking pan and press evenly into bottom.

3   Bake until crust is firm, about 15 minutes.

4   While crust is baking, combine rhubarb, granulated sugar, cornstarch, and orange juice in a saucepan. Cook over medium heat while stirring until mixture comes to a boil and thickens. Remove from heat and stir in vanilla. Let cool slightly.

5   When crust is baked, remove from oven and pour rhubarb filling over hot crust. Sprinkle the remaining streusel over fruit to cover completely and press down lightly to form an even layer.

6   Return to oven and bake until topping is browned and firm to the touch, about 30 minutes. Place pan on a rack to cool; cut into 2½″ × 2″ bars.

Makes about 12 cookies.

Store cookies covered in the baking pan in refrigerator for up to four days. Do not freeze.

Here's a scrumptious brownie-style bar cookie,
wloaded with milk chocolate, streaks of melting
marshmallows, and crunchy walnuts.

Rocky Road Cookies

6 ounces milk chocolate, cut into pieces

¼ cup (½ stick) unsalted butter, cut into pieces

2 large eggs

1 cup all-purpose flour

¼ teaspoon baking soda

¼ teaspoon salt

1 cup milk chocolate chips

1 cup miniature marshmallows

1 cup coarsely chopped walnuts

1   Heat oven to 325°F.

2   Melt chocolate and butter in the top of a double boiler over barely simmering water. Or, place in a microwavable dish and melt in microwave set on medium power for 2½ minutes. Remove from heat, stir until smooth, and set aside.

3   In a mixing bowl, beat eggs until foamy. Add melted chocolate mixture and blend until smooth.

4   In a separate bowl, mix flour, baking soda, and salt. Add to chocolate mixture and blend. Stir in chocolate chips, marshmallows, and walnuts. (Batter will be thick and stiff.) Pour into a greased 9-inch square baking pan and spread evenly.

5   Bake until cookies are browned and firm to the touch, about 25 minutes. Place pan on a rack to cool; cut into 2½" × 2" bars.

Makes about 12 bar cookies.

Store cookies covered in the baking pan at room temperature for up to three days.

These bar cookies are a delightful
way to enjoy the exotic flavor of
the crimson-toned persimmon.

Sweet Persimmon Fireside Cookies

2 cups all-purpose flour

½ cup cake flour

1 teaspoon cinnamon

1 teaspoon ginger

½ teaspoon baking soda

¼ teaspoon salt

½ cup (1 stick) unsalted butter, at room temperature

1 cup granulated sugar

Grated rind of 1 lemon

1 cup pureed ripe persimmon pulp (about 2 medium persimmons)

1 large egg

¼ cup confectioners' sugar

1 Heat oven to 375°F.

2 Combine both flours, cinnamon, ginger, baking soda, and salt in a bowl. Set aside.

3 In a separate bowl, cream butter, granulated sugar, and lemon rind until fluffy and smooth. Add persimmon pulp and egg and blend.

4 Gradually add flour mixture and mix until blended. Pour batter into a greased 9″ × 13″ baking pan and spread out evenly.

5 Bake until cookies are golden brown and a cake tester inserted in the center comes out clean, about 25 minutes. Place pan on a rack and let cool; sift confectioners' sugar evenly over the top and cut into 3″ × 2″ bars.

Makes about 16 bar cookies.

Store cookies covered in the baking pan at room temperature for up to three days.

4

Holiday

COOKIES

These almond caramel slices are similar to holiday favorites called Florentines. Loaded with almonds and buttery caramel, these easy-to-eat cookies are sensual, yet not too sweet. They are even better the day after they are baked.

Almond Caramel Slices

¾ cup (1½ sticks) unsalted butter, at room temperature

⅓ cup plus ¼ cup granulated sugar

1 large egg, separated

1 cup all-purpose flour

¼ cup packed dark brown sugar

2 tablespoons light corn syrup

½ cup whipping cream

½ teaspoon vanilla extract

1½ cups sliced almonds

1   Heat oven to 350°F.

2   In a mixing bowl, cream ½ cup (1 stick) of the butter with the ⅓ cup granulated sugar until smooth.

3   Add egg yolk and flour, mixing to form dough. Press evenly into bottom of ungreased 8-inch square baking pan. Beat egg white in a small bowl until frothy. Brush over dough, using as much as necessary to coat liberally.

4   Bake until lightly golden, 15–20 minutes. Place on a rack to cool.

5   Meanwhile, combine the remaining ¼ cup butter and ¼ cup sugar with the brown sugar, corn syrup, and whipping cream in a saucepan. Bring mixture to boil over medium heat, stirring to dissolve sugars. Boil 3 minutes. Remove from heat and stir in vanilla and almonds. Pour and spread topping evenly over crust.

6   Return to oven and bake until topping is bubbling all over, about 10 minutes. Place pan on a rack to cool; cut into 2½″ × 1½″ slices.

Makes about 15 cookies.

Store cookies covered in the baking pan at room temperature for up to five days. Do not freeze.

Fruit-topped cookies add welcome variety to traditional
holiday dessert trays. This cookie has the wonderful appeal
of a real home-baked pie, yet it can be eaten with your fingers.

Apple Pie Bars

2 cups all-purpose flour

1 cup confectioners' sugar

½ cup ground walnuts

1 cup (2 sticks) unsalted butter, slightly softened, cut into pieces

2 large eggs

3 large sweet apples (such as Gala or Fuji), peeled, cored, and
   chopped

¼ cup water

½ cup packed dark brown sugar

1 teaspoon cinnamon

1 cup sour cream

1   Heat oven to 350°F.

2   Combine flour, confectioners' sugar, and walnuts in a bowl. Cut in butter until mixture is crumbly. Add 1 egg and mix to form dough. Press evenly into bottom of ungreased 9″ × 13″ baking pan.

3   Bake until lightly golden, about 20 minutes. Place on a rack to cool.

4   Meanwhile, place apples in a microwavable dish and drizzle with water. Cover dish with plastic wrap and cook apples in microwave set on high power for 4 to 5 minutes, until tender. Drain apples and let cool slightly. Combine with brown sugar and cinnamon in bowl, stirring well. Spread evenly over baked crust.

5   Combine sour cream and remaining egg in bowl, mixing to blend smoothly. Spread evenly over apple topping. Return to oven and bake until topping is set but not browned, about 25 minutes. Place pan on a rack and let cool; cut into 2-inch squares. Serve at room temperature.

Makes about 24 cookies.

Store cookies covered in the baking pan in refrigerator for up to three days. Bring back to room temperature to serve. Do not freeze.

In this decadent and delicious bar cookie, you have three luscious layers of chocolate to sink your teeth into: a dark chocolate cookie crust, a creamy chocolate filling, and a silken white chocolate truffle topping. These would make a welcome hostess gift during the holiday season.

Chocolate Truffle Triangles

¾ cup (1½ sticks) plus 2 tablespoons unsalted butter, at room temperature

½ cup plus 2 tablespoons granulated sugar

1 large egg yolk

½ teaspoon vanilla extract

1 cup all-purpose flour

¼ cup Dutch-processed cocoa powder

8 ounces semisweet chocolate, cut into pieces

⅓ cup espresso or strong coffee, hot

8 ounces white chocolate, cut into pieces

⅔ cup whipping cream

1 Heat oven to 375°F.

2 In a mixing bowl, cream ½ cup (1 stick) of butter with ½ cup sugar until smooth. Add egg yolk and vanilla.

3   Add flour and cocoa. Mix until dough forms. Spread and press dough evenly into an ungreased 8-inch square baking pan.

4   Bake until firm to the touch, about 10 minutes. Place on a rack to cool.

5   Melt semisweet chocolate with ¼ cup (½ stick) butter in saucepan. Stir to blend and set aside.

6   Stir the 2 tablespoons of sugar into the hot espresso until dissolved. Cool to warm and stir into melted chocolate mixture. Cool filling in refrigerator just until spreadable. Spread evenly onto baked cookie crust in pan. Chill pan in refrigerator until filling is set, 2–3 hours.

7   Place white chocolate in a mixing bowl. Bring cream to boil in a saucepan, remove from heat, and pour over white chocolate while stirring with wire whisk to blend. Whisk in remaining 2 tablespoons of butter. Cool topping in refrigerator just until spreadable.

8   Spread white truffle topping evenly over chocolate filling. Chill pan in refrigerator until topping is set, 2–3 hours. Cut into 2½-inch squares, then cut each square diagonally in half into a triangle.

Makes about 12 cookies.

Store cookies covered in the baking pan in refrigerator for up to five days. Do not freeze.

Typically a Jewish holiday treat, rugelach are delightful all year round and for any occasion. This is a classic rendition of tender, flaky pastry filled with fruit jam, raisins, cinnamon, and walnuts and formed into a crescent shape. But watch out, these cookies are habit forming.

Cinnamon Walnut Rugelach

1½ cups all-purpose flour

2½ tablespoons plus ¼ cup granulated sugar

¼ teaspoon salt

½ cup (1 stick) unsalted butter, slightly softened, cut into pieces

1 large egg, separated

½ cup sour cream

¼ cup Damson plum preserves

¼ teaspoon cinnamon

⅓ cup golden raisins

½ cup coarsely chopped walnuts

1 Combine flour, 2 tablespoons of sugar (reserving ½ tablespoon for garnish), and salt in a bowl. Cut in butter until mixture is crumbly.

2   Stir the egg yolk into sour cream. Add to flour mixture to form a soft dough. Wrap dough in plastic wrap and refrigerate for at least 1 hour.

3   Heat oven to 350°F.

4   Divide chilled dough in half and roll each piece out on a lightly floured surface to a 10-inch circle. Spread half (2 tablespoons) of plum preserves evenly onto each circle of dough.

5   Combine ¼ cup of the granulated sugar with cinnamon. Sprinkle each circle of dough with half the cinnamon-sugar, then sprinkle with half the raisins and half the walnuts. Press down lightly to form an even layer.

6   Cut each circle of dough into 8 pie-shaped wedges. Starting at the wide end, roll each wedge of dough tightly around filling to form a crescent shaped cookie.

7   Arrange crescents on greased or nonstick cookie sheets, pointed-end down and spaced 1½ inches apart. Brush tops with the egg white, beaten until frothy, and sprinkle lightly with the remaining sugar.

8   Bake until cookies are golden, about 30 minutes. Using a spatula, transfer cookies to a rack and let cool.

Makes about 16 cookies.

Store cookies in an airtight jar or tin at room temperature for up to five days.

Cream cheese and sour cream moisten and enrich this rugelach
dough to produce a cookie with a long shelf life. Marmalade is an
unusual and intriguing filling for this popular cookie.

Citrus Rugelach

½ cup (1 stick) unsalted butter, at room temperature

4 ounces cream cheese, at room temperature

½ cup sour cream

1½ cups all-purpose flour

½ cup orange marmalade

2 tablespoons orange blossom honey

⅔ cup chopped walnuts

1 egg white, lightly beaten

1 tablespoon granulated sugar

1 Heat oven to 350°F.

2 In a mixing bowl, cream butter and cream cheese together until smooth. Add sour cream and blend.

3 Add flour and mix to form soft dough. Divide dough in half. Roll each half out onto a lightly floured surface to a 14″ × 7″ rectangle.

4 Combine marmalade and honey in a small bowl. Spread half the mixture evenly onto each rectangle of dough. Sprinkle ⅓ cup walnuts over each. Beginning with long side, roll dough up around filling, jelly-roll fashion, into a narrow log.

5 Brush each log of dough with beaten egg white and sprinkle with sugar. Cut crosswise into 2-inch wide slices. Arrange cookies, cut-side down, on greased or nonstick cookie sheets, spacing them 1 inch apart.

6 Bake until golden, about 30 minutes. Using a spatula, transfer cookies to a rack and let cool.

Makes about 14 cookies.

Store cookies in an airtight jar or tin at room temperature for up to five days.

Save some holiday eggnog for these wonderful cookies.
Rum-spiked icing and a bit of nutmeg enhance the eggnog flavor.

Eggnog Cookies with Rum Butter Icing

½ cup (1 stick) unsalted butter, at room temperature

1 cup packed dark brown sugar

1 large egg

⅔ cup eggnog

2 cups all-purpose flour

½ teaspoon baking soda

½ teaspoon salt

½ teaspoon nutmeg

½ teaspoon ginger

Rum Butter Icing (recipe follows)

¼ teaspoon nutmeg, for garnish

1 Heat oven to 350°F.

2 In a mixing bowl, cream butter and brown sugar until smooth. Add egg and blend; add eggnog.

150

3   In a separate bowl, mix flour, baking soda, salt, and spices. Add to the creamed mixture. Blend until smooth.

4   Using either an individual ¼-cup measure or a 2-ounce ice-cream scoop, scoop level measures of dough and drop 2½ inches apart onto ungreased cookie sheets.

5   Bake until cookies are golden and firm to the touch, about 15 minutes. Using a spatula, transfer cookies to a rack and let cool.

6   When cookies are completely cool, ice with Rum Butter Icing. Garnish each cookie with a sprinkle of nutmeg.

RUM BUTTER ICING	
	¼ cup (½ stick) unsalted butter
	3 tablespoons rum, light or dark
	1½ cups confectioners' sugar

1   Melt butter and combine with rum in mixing bowl. Stir in sugar, ½ cup at a time, blending until smooth. Set aside at least 15 minutes to thicken slightly.

2   Spread icing onto tops of cooled cookies.

Makes about 14 cookies.

Store cookies in an airtight tin at room temperature for up to three days.

A delightful combination of spices and the gentle flavor of molasses make these cookies distinctively delicious. They are sure to become real favorites at holiday time.

Ginger Cookies

1½ cups all-purpose flour

¾ cup cake flour

1 teaspoon baking soda

½ teaspoon salt

1 teaspoon ginger

½ teaspoon cinnamon

½ teaspoon ground cloves

¾ cup (1½ sticks) unsalted butter, at room temperature

¾ cup packed dark brown sugar

¼ cup dark molasses

2 tablespoons milk

1 large egg

¼ cup granulated sugar

1   Combine both flours with the baking soda, salt, and spices in a bowl. Set aside.

2   In a separate bowl, cream butter and brown sugar until fluffy and smooth. Add molasses, milk, and egg and blend. Add flour mixture and blend. Cover dough with plastic wrap and refrigerate for at least 1 hour.

3   Heat oven to 375°F.

4   To form each cookie, roll 3 tablespoons of chilled dough into a ball. Pour the granulated sugar onto a plate. Roll each dough ball into the sugar to coat all sides. Place on ungreased cookie sheets and flatten into 3-inch rounds, spacing them 2 inches apart.

5   Bake until cookies are firm to the touch and tops are slightly cracked, about 10 minutes. (Do not overbake.) Remove cookies from oven and let them set for 2 minutes. Using a spatula, transfer cookies to a rack and let cool.

Makes about 17 cookies.

Store cookies in an airtight plastic storage bag at room temperature for up to three days.

The spicy aroma of freshly baked gingerbread is among the most pleasant and familiar of holiday smells. These decorated gingerbread men, though meant to be eaten, can also be left out to harden and used as ornaments.

Iced Gingerbread Men

2½ cups all-purpose flour

1 teaspoon baking soda

1 teaspoon ginger

1 teaspoon cinnamon

½ teaspoon ground cloves

½ teaspoon salt

⅛ teaspoon black pepper

1 cup (2 sticks) unsalted butter, at room temperature

1 cup packed dark brown sugar

2 large eggs

½ cup strong coffee, at room temperature

½ cup dark molasses

½ cup light corn syrup

Icing (recipe follows)

1 Heat oven to 350°F.

2 Combine flour, baking soda, spices, salt, and pepper in a bowl. Set aside.

3 In a separate bowl, cream butter and brown sugar until smooth. Add eggs; then add coffee, molasses, and corn syrup and blend. Add the flour mixture and stir to form stiff dough.

4 Grease the 5″ × 3″ × ¾″ molds of a gingerbread pan. Scoop 3 level tablespoons of batter into each mold and spread evenly to fill the space.

5 Bake until an inserted toothpick comes out clean, about 15 minutes. Unmold from pan while warm, about 5 minutes out of oven, onto a wire rack to cool. Clean and regrease pan to bake remaining cookies.

6 When cookies are completely cool, frost with icing.

ICING	
	3 cups confectioners' sugar
	2 egg whites, beaten slightly
	1 teaspoon lemon juice

1 In a bowl, stir together all ingredients until smooth. Consistency should be thick but pourable.

2 Pipe icing through pastry bag to decorate cooled cookies.

Makes about 18 cookies.

To prevent hardening, wrap each cookie individually in plastic wrap and store at room temperature for up to three days.

Count on these delicate, heavenly puffs to
disappear quickly. For a distinct holiday look,
add food coloring to the icing.

Lemon Puffs

½ cup (1 stick) unsalted butter, at room temperature

½ cup granulated sugar

3 large eggs

2 cups all-purpose flour

1 tablespoon baking powder

1½ tablespoons lemon juice

Grated rind of 1 lemon (about 1 teaspoon)

Icing (recipe follows)

1   Heat oven to 375°F.

2   In a mixing bowl, cream butter and sugar until fluffy and smooth. Add eggs, one at a time, and blend.

3   In a separate bowl, sift together flour and baking powder. Add to creamed mixture; then add lemon juice and rind, blending until smooth.

4   Scoop 2 level tablespoons of dough and roll to form each cookie. Place onto ungreased cookie sheets, spacing 2 inches apart.

5   Bake until cookies are lightly golden, about 15 minutes. Using a spatula, transfer cookies to a rack and let cool.

6   When cookies are completely cool, frost with icing.

ICING

2 cups confectioners' sugar

¼ cup freshly squeezed lemon juice (1 lemon)

1   Place sugar in a bowl. Whisk in the lemon juice until smooth. Set aside for at least 5 minutes to set slightly.

2   Spoon icing evenly onto tops of cooled cookies.

Makes about 14 cookies.

Store cookies in an airtight jar or tin at room temperature for up to three days.

Pretty as they are to look at, these cookies taste even
better and will be big hits during holiday celebrations. Serve
them while they're still slightly warm from the oven.

Marbled Cheesecake Squares

2 cups plus 1 tablespoon all-purpose flour

½ cup packed dark brown sugar

½ cup (1 stick) unsalted butter, slightly softened

16 ounces cream cheese, at room temperature

¾ cup granulated sugar

3 large eggs

1 teaspoon vanilla extract

3 tablespoons whipping cream

4 ounces semisweet chocolate, melted

1   Heat oven to 350°F.

2   Combine 2 cups of flour and brown sugar in a mixing bowl. Cut in butter until mixture is crumbly. Spread and pat firmly into bottom of an ungreased 9″ × 13″ baking pan.

3   Bake until lightly browned, about 15 minutes. Place pan on a rack to cool and lower oven temperature to 325°F.

4   Combine cream cheese and sugar in mixing bowl. Beat until fluffy and smooth; add eggs one at a time. Stir in remaining tablespoon of flour along with the vanilla and whipping cream.

5   Pour batter evenly onto baked crust. Spoon melted chocolate over topping. Using a table knife, swirl the chocolate through the cheese topping until marbled throughout.

6   Return to oven and bake until center is set, about 35 minutes. Place pan on a rack to cool; cut into 2-inch squares. Serve slightly warm, at room temperature, or chilled.

Makes about 24 squares.

Store covered in the baking pan at room temperature for one day and in the refrigerator for up to five days.

Surprise the trick-or-treat crowd with
these decorative, seasonal cookies.

Pumpkin Cookies with Cream Cheese Frosting

2 cups all-purpose flour

1 teaspoon baking powder

1 teaspoon baking soda

1 teaspoon salt

2 teaspoons cinnamon

½ teaspoon ginger

½ teaspoon nutmeg

½ teaspoon ground cloves

1 cup (2 sticks) unsalted butter, at room temperature

1 cup granulated sugar

1 cup canned solid-pack pumpkin

1 large egg

1 teaspoon vanilla extract

Cream Cheese Frosting (recipe follows)

1   Heat oven to 350°F.

2   Combine flour, baking powder, baking soda, salt, and spices in a bowl. Set aside.

3   In a mixing bowl, cream butter and sugar until fluffy and smooth. Add pumpkin, egg, and vanilla and blend. Stir in flour mixture.

4   Scoop 2 level tablespoons of dough and roll to form each cookie. Place onto greased or nonstick cookie sheets, spacing them 2 inches apart. Bake until cookies are lightly browned, about 15 minutes. They will feel slightly soft to touch. Using a spatula, transfer cookies to a rack and let cool.

5   When completely cool, frost with Cream Cheese Frosting.

CREAM CHEESE FROSTING

8 ounces cream cheese, at room temperature

¼ cup (½ stick) unsalted butter, at room temperature

1 cup confectioners' sugar

1   Beat cream cheese and butter in a mixer until smooth. Add sugar slowly to blend.

2   Spread frosting onto cookies or pipe through pastry bag.

Makes about 20 cookies.

Store cookies in a loosely covered container at room temperature for up to three days.